This Construction Life

First published 2019

Published under licence by The Self-Publishing Partnership,
7 Green Park Station, Bath BA1 1JB

ISBN printed book: 978-1-83952-036-5
ISBN e-book: 978-1-83952-037-2

Cover design by Kevin Rylands
Internal design by Andrew Easton

This book is printed on FSC certified paper

Printed by CPI Group (UK) Ltd, Croydon CR0 4YY

PATRICK
BUTLER

Chapter 1

THE BEGINNING... A DIFFERENT WORLD! SEEMS LIKE CENTURIES AGO

I have to go back in time a bit... The story starts in the 1970s in Ireland. 1974, to be exact.

It was a year full of uncertainty, donkey jackets and flares. Disco was in its infancy. Then there was world unrest. Middle Eastern meddling and division. Oil embargoes led to shortages of fuel at the petrol pumps. It was the year of lining up. The Irish population lined up in their cars to get fuel, if there was enough to go around. The fuel was being rationed to breaking point. The Garda were having to intervene to avert civil unrest. People lined up for long periods and were rationed even basic building materials like cement. Production of cement depended on oil. More like a Communist country than a democratic one. Something to do with the United States backing the Israeli government in the Arab-Israeli War. It still rages on today! The oil cartel, OPEC, tried to punish the United States for taking the Israeli side. This really affected the Western world. Ireland was no exception. We bought our oil internationally. Britain had problems, too. The British Army were on standby to man the oil tankers to deliver fuel if the civilian blockades didn't stop. Real serious stuff!

It was also a year of strikes by many unions in Ireland. Living standards dropped due to the economy stalling. Inflation was partly to blame. People were striking over pay and conditions. The previous decade of the 1960s was an energised decade. In the 60s everything was rebellion, free love, fun, harmony and the attitude we can do anything we want. The era of The Beatles, The Rolling Stones, showbands, rock n' roll, Top of the Pops, mini-skirts and drainpipe trousers. The decade of great music, fashion, sunny days and good times. The decade of the television. This box in the corner of your living room changed everything. The power of that medium was electric. The 60s for a young teen or 20-something were times full of enthusiasm and fun.

This global phenomenon of great music, psychedelic times and this amazing energy. Britain was at the forefront of it. Ireland looked up to big brother Britain for trends and style. Our nation loved the cool trends that emerged from Britain in those decades. The attitude of the young was: We don't have to uphold the conservative ways of our fathers and mothers. We will do what we want anyway. They were right! Live for the moment and have as much fun as you can while your conservative parents are not looking. This was my parents' era. They tell me it was a fabulous time.

Then the 1970s arrived. The age of open drug-taking and the psychedelic living of the 1960s had come to an abrupt end. It was a time of upheaval, not to mention the Troubles in Northern Ireland. There were political, social and religious divisions. Political dialogue was frayed between the Irish and

British governments. It was a complicated problem. In Northern Ireland, people who had allegiance to the Crown were not willing to give up power and those with no power were hungry to get a balance, voting rights and job equality. Complex! Peace in Northern Ireland was a distant hope. A tough time for all people who lived there. A real scary time for anyone living on the island of Ireland or on the border, for that matter. Reality had just stepped in and taken hold with force. We lived in the South and didn't have to bear the full brunt of war. It was, however, a tense period. Unemployment was high and bank robberies were on the rise. Sometimes driven by terrorists. The terrorists from both sides of the divide didn't stop there. They used to kidnap rich business people for ransom money. These years were not boring by any standard. The evening news almost always had a headline story of people being shot or bombed in Northern Ireland. But it was reported on so often it was sort of normalised. The place where all this trouble was going on was about 200 miles away from where we lived as the crow flies, and there was a border between us. It just seemed it was far away. I can't imagine the pain of living in a place with so much trouble.

Ireland in the 1970s

THE BEGINNING... A DIFFERENT WORLD! SEEMS LIKE CENTURIES AGO

In the South of Ireland money was delivered to the banks by armoured truck with an Army and police escort. Real guns were cocked by Army personnel at the doors of banks to ensure safe delivery of money on a Thursday or Friday. The Army was a real active domestic service at that time. A troop of Army Land Rover Defenders and a police escort of the Brink's armoured truck were normal. You would arrive at the bank just after lunch on, say, a Friday to collect wages and then this big entourage would arrive. You were aware they were present but you accepted it as the norm. A little tense but normal!

You also had to have two people when going to the bank to collect the cash. At that time, people were paid their wages in a wage packet that contained cash. The bank would not give you a large sum of cash without a second person present. We accepted this as normal procedure. By today's standards you would think that it was more like Venezuela than Ireland. One thing is for sure, money did go further in those times for us kids. Having said that, inflation in the mid-70s was rising and people's pockets were being squeezed, hence the unrest. Money did have a certain amount of buying power.

That was the year I was born, 1974. A hard year economically and politically. "Waterloo" by Abba was no. 1 in the charts. Born on a Saturday. They say Saturday's child works hard for a living. That is exactly what happened!

I am convinced that this very statement is a fact. I was destined to be a hard worker. The family were pupils of the school of hard work. A trait that was enforced by the family rules. A family business with rules. I suppose I was very lucky. Lucky to be born Irish. Lucky to get that tough schooling. Lucky to have that get-up-and-go.

That's the thing I am most grateful for in life. I was born

in Ireland. A great country to be brought up in and educated. Ireland has a good-quality education system. An Ireland not free from its own set of problems, but good at educating its young! Whether people felt they had to emigrate or not, Ireland no doubt was the mother country with many great and wonderful attributes. Home! This is where I started out in life and this is where I first met characters.

Whether they were school characters, construction characters or just other characters. I met them all! People of all shapes and sizes. Talented people from all over the world. People with their stories and life experiences. Great, decent, honest, tough, wonderful, naughty, aloof and downright despicable. Starting with construction in the 1970s and right through to 30 years later. I have picked a few stories that I remembered. But first I will paint a picture of life in the 1970s and 1980s in Ireland. The 1970s being years of strikes and unrest. The 1980s followed on as a decade marred with recession and mass emigration from Ireland. It was closed in many respects. The economy was in bad shape. My old man didn't sell one house in about seven years during the 1980s; in 1983 they had to close the gates for a period which hurt everyone. It was a tough decade. Anyone who got a third-level education would up and leave and pursue a career abroad. Many never returned. Many without that level of education never returned either. Leaving Ireland was a heavy burden for families. Most people never had that relationship again with their families once they left Ireland.

Ireland
THE BEGINNING... A WORKING MAN IN CONSTRUCTION IN IRELAND IN THE 1970s

Just to give you a snippet of the life of an Irishman working in construction in the 1970s. By today's standards using the word "man" in the last sentence would be wrong but in the 1970s in Ireland women didn't work on sites. Life as a construction worker in Ireland was tough in this decade. Working as a mason, plasterer or labouring man for that matter was tough in Ireland in those years. It was a wet, damp country and construction was a **very heavy,** labour-intensive industry. Structures were constructed in masonry and materials were heavy. A tough place to work, "this game". Note I say "game". It was far from a game. The men were tough nuts. Some uncivilised. You left your feelings at home if you worked on a building site. Men didn't mince their words. You had to be a tough guy to survive this environment. Many of the men were in the game, out of being born into it. They were in that family of painters, carpenters, bricklayers, plasterers or whatever. Steps of the stairs they were coming to work. Sometimes from the great-grandfather to the great-grandson. Proud people.

The labouring men sometimes came from farming backgrounds and others came from the working classes in the city, as did the tradesmen. You would have to be a tough man to be a foreman that time. Men would work alright because there were plenty to replace you. Sometimes they would be militant. In a rising tide they would be demanding better money. They would want to try and break a foreman. Men were real pups then. They would always be seeking out a man's weakness to see if they could break him. A foreman would be better to sack a few every now and then to keep them on their toes. One thing I do remember was that there was great manual production on-site. Men produced a large amount of hard labour in eight hours. Never to be equalled manually again on-site.

In Ireland there was a system of an advance on your wages known as "The Sub". This was a normal part of construction culture. This would be requested from the construction company boss by an employee on a Monday morning or sometimes a Tuesday morning. They might miss Monday! Most construction company bosses would have had a "sub pocket" sewn into their trousers. This pocket would contain different denomination banknotes. The drink culture in Ireland was a phenomenon that many tradesmen and labourers upheld. A few didn't know when to quit! They spent all their money on alcohol at the weekend and would ask for "The Sub" on Monday to carry them over for the week. There were pubs called early houses that would open on a Monday morning to cater for all the weekend hangovers. Some would leave the wives short of money. Life was hard for some and the work was hard, too.

It rained like hell there for about two-thirds of the year. It was always raining and dull in autumn, winter and sometimes spring. OK. You can get good sunny weather there, too, but it never lasts too long. Being right beside the Atlantic Ocean brings weather systems. Being honest, Ireland has the freshest air in the whole world. A moderate climate and the most beautiful scenic country in the world with the greenest fields and picturesque rolling hills but, if you are working in a labour-intensive outdoor job, well, it's not exactly the Ritz, is it?

"The Sub" would come at a cost. The company would deduct the "sub money" from the person at the end of the week it was requested. Construction also had a pay system called "wet time". It was also a part of construction life. You received more money if you worked in the rain. Arthritis would be a common complaint by construction workers and farmers as a result of working in such conditions. This system died out in the 1980s. I worked in the rain, too. You have to work in the rain in Ireland. Otherwise you will get nothing done. I admit, it takes its toll. Creaky knees and elbow joints. Running up gantries with two full buckets of mortar or ten bricks in a brick clamp in each hand. Yes, that's 20 bricks at a time.

I know it wasn't exactly the industrial era of the 1870s but it was still a hard industry. If you get out of bed every morning for a month at a time and it's raining, well, that does tend to grind you down. They say people get sick of the sun all the time. Well, try the rain! Try it carrying an extra few kilos in wet clothes and muck-laden wellies. Work on a site where it has been raining for a month. The muck would be 4 inches thick under your wellingtons and your coat would be about 10kgs heavier with water from the rain. I hated the oilskins. They would always leak into your underpants or vest. Then you would sweat inside the damn things. You might as well be in a bath of Vaseline. Shite! 50kgs would be an average weight of most materials at that time. Add the weight of the rain and the mud. Then you are starting to look windswept.

The machinery was cumbersome. A point I will mention again, no doubt. The Thwaites Dumpers pumping out black thick diesel fumes and no hydraulics on the tipper. Just YouTube these dumpers and you will see what I mean. It was a job to start them on a freezing cold morning. A good warm-up for you to kill the frozen tops of your fingers. Then as the day would thaw out you might be working in a house with no roof yet and the water would be dripping off the joists. Traipsing around the floors with the slosh of water below your feet. Water was everywhere. We accepted it as part of life. I look back and think that it must have been hard for those men. Life was definitely tougher for them. Some men lived to a ripe old age and some died young from it. I salute you, "the men in the flat caps who went before me". You were brilliant. This book is a tribute to that life, highlighting what life was like then with a bit of comedy thrown in the mix and how life evolved for me. I remembered just a few stories.

My family owned this construction company that built these estates of luxury homes in Ireland. This is where it all started for me. For me life was mapped out early. The early years living in a house at the top of a new and progressing housing estate of houses. I watched on as the construction of rows and rows of detached and semi-detached houses were constructed. It was already in my blood. I was being primed for a life less than ordinary. I was going to be walking the line, too! I was soon to enter the world of grey, pissy building sites, too. It was only a matter of time. But first we hit the schoolboy years!

Ireland in the 1980s

Early schoolboy years in Ireland: my life, our era

In the 1980s you go to school and do the normal stuff like any other kid. Play hurling or football, do your homework and generally behave yourself. Being seen and not heard was a must. Cycle your BMX bike or Peugeot racer around the locality. Get on the merry-go-rounds in the tarmac-surfaced playground and push your friends on it at breakneck speed with the hope that you would throw them off the damn thing. All fun stuff! All it would bring you was a grazed knee or cut on the palm of your hand. Nothing serious and your mother wouldn't be suing the council either. You got a clip on the ear and a warning that you were not to do it again. You were a bloody eejit for trying it. That's the thing I do not understand today. Kids are cotton-woolled today! That rubber matting is not thick enough or my Johnny hurt his hand etc… Then there is an enquiry. Why? Why not let kids be kids?

The thing was none of us died from falling on that tarmac or from riding your bike down a hill as fast as you could on the wrong side of the road. It was all a part of being a kid in urban Ireland. Being a daredevil was a badge of honour. If you did come into contact with a car – by that I mean slam into the fender and it was, say, "Mr Murphy your eighty-year-old neighbour" who happened to come around the corner slowly – you would say, Sorry Mr Murphy, keep going and your friends would all scarper.

We would all meet up a few hundred metres away and have a big laugh and someone else would do it. Then it was a waiting game. Would the old codger report you to your parents or not! He was so old that he probably didn't even know he was in the car or driving for that matter. Most of the time you would get away with an incident like it. Smoking, on the other hand, was forbidden. If you were caught smoking that was a serious matter. That was an offence that cost you your liberty. Being grounded for a month. You would probably have to tell the priest in confession. The habit of smoking never interested me. Peer pressure never bothered me. I liked doing my own thing. If my friends all headed left, I went right. I was just happy being a kid playing on the road with friends. We were free and life was easy on the mind.

We would run around the road playing a game called TIG or hide-and-seek with your friends in the cold autumn days with just a T-shirt and flared trousers on you. Your mother would be giving you the third degree about catching your death of cold. She would be ranting and raving that she would not be bringing you to the doctor if you got a cold. We rarely got sick and we didn't even feel the cold. That was primary school. Primary school was all good except a bollix of a teacher who had sadistic tendencies. This is when I was about nine years old. Beating young, defenceless kids was one of his vices. A real psycho. He would call the same usual suspects every day knowing he had the shit scared out of them and the kids would answer every question wrongly out of fear. Some kids pissed in their pants. He would hit you hard in the guts. A bandy walk and jam jars of glasses. A real beauty. Brad Pitt not! The sunshine in all this was that after the age of nine I hadn't to endure that fellow ever again. He gave me a good few beatings. I didn't tell my parents because I thought I was the one that was wrong. My parents were shocked 20 years later when I told them about that guy. You can't change the past!

Like most kids of that era we had games. We didn't have technology so we had to interact with each other and engineer games ourselves. Collective thoughts can lead to untold mischief, spin the bottle being a fun adolescent game. This was a game where boys and girls sit in a circle and put a bottle in the middle of the group. Everyone gets a chance to spin the bottle.

Wherever the bottle STOPS you have to kiss that person. Quite an interesting way to learn how to kiss. A way to find out who is a slobber of a kisser and who is smooth. I often had saliva from my forehead to my chin by some young girl trying to suck my face off. Not that I was complaining! We were quite innocent. It was a forbidden element to our life. My parents or the girl's parents wouldn't like that we were getting up to mischief. It was real fun stuff. Harmless fun. We were finding ourselves and who we were. Life was constantly evolving. The age of innocence and discovery!

The only thing about this kind of fun stuff is that if the people, i.e. boy and girl, got carried away and, well, you know, and that girl got pregnant, well, that would be a scandal. The whole neighbourhood would have it. Lots of tongue-wagging and gossip. It was totally unacceptable to have a child out of wedlock in Ireland. The Church would be poking their noses in, too! That scenario is another story for another book.

Ireland in the 1980s

TEENAGE YEARS!

This was the picture of a kid growing up in the 1980s. At age 12 I started taking a real interest in music. The 80s music bands like The Cure (Robert Smith with that weird hair and make-up), Queen, A-ha, Bros, The Smiths, Howard Jones, Frankie Goes to Hollywood, Guns N' Roses, Dire Straits, AC/DC, U2, Alison Moyet, Depeche Mode, China Crisis, Spandau Ballet, and many more. All with funny haircuts, parka jackets. Music synthesisers and the age of technology was born. The Commodore 64 computer and the Atari games console. My cousin who ended up being a whizz in the computer industry had a Commodore 64. My friend had an Atari games console. BMX bikes were great. Then there was the sweetshop where you could get your daily fix of sweets for between 10 and 20 pence. Don't mention the fillings and the trips to the dentist.

Jim had a convenience shop near where I lived. Every child in the locality got their sweets from Jim. He looked after his parents who were close to 90 at the time. God bless them, we thought they were ancient. Jim was a nice fellow. He was a decent sort. He wore jam jar glasses with black rims. He had a lot of stuff. By that I mean SWEETS. Jim's shop was demolished this year, 2019. This for me was the loss of an institution. A place where friends met, hung out and in some cases while one kid distracted him, another robbed a bar of chocolate.

Jim had every sweet you could imagine. The penny sweets. Black Jacks, Fruit Salads, penny jellies, Fish 'n' Chips white chocolate, Milk Teeth, Refreshers, gobstoppers, Cola bottles and many more. A Lucky Bag was 7p. A Fizzy Cola Lolly was 5p, and if you got a lucky number 7 on the inside of the wrapper, you got a free lolly. A bag of Tayto crisps for 12p. Monster Munch was 13p. A Big Time bar was, I think, 7p. It was 30p for a bottle of Shannonside orange, raspberry, lime or cream soda. They tasted fantastic! A blast of flavour all multiplied by 200% and probably artificially flavoured.

The introduction of that WHAM bar for 13p. Oh my God! The introduction of crackling candy to our taste buds with a sour strawberry flavour. A euphoric experience. Epic! The WHAM bars took a while to eat and you would be gnawing them up and down and over and back in your mouth to eventually break a piece off it. The big-time bars were the same. A bar of toffee with smooth, silky chocolate on the outside. In the fridge there was Mr. Freeze, a frozen sweet sugar, big, plastic tube. You bit the end off and then sucked on it. They cost 7p. Then there was a Brunch, orange split ice cream, a Wibbly Wobbly Wonder, loop de loop, Big Foots, Iceberg and a Maxi Twist. They were all about 20p. Jim was a dentist's dream!

We as kids might have 20p maybe once or twice a week if we were very lucky. So anytime this happened it was into Jim's shop. A pound note was a FORTUNE of money to us at 12 years of age. The problem for our parents was that we passed Jim's shop every day after school. The temptation was always in our path. If my mother said don't go into Jim's shop that translated to, go into Jim's shop but don't let me find out. One particular year, I think it was 1985, I went to the shop with 20p.

I took a Mr. Freeze out of the fridge which was 7p and then asked Jim for a packet of Monster Munch which was 13p. Jim said that they had gone up to 14p. They had gone up in price by a penny. I said I had only 20p. Well, it's one or the other, he responded. I had to go out of the shop without the Monster Munch crisps. I was gutted! I remember that was a bombshell to me. That really burst my bubble and I remembered it forever. That one penny price hike!

We had simple things to keep us occupied those times. One such game was conker battles. On the way home from school, we used to collect conkers off the ground after they fell from Horse Chestnut trees. We would get a nail and put a hole in them. Then we would put a string through the hole and tie a knot in it. Then we would spar with another kid and try break his conker with our conker. If you broke his conker you got a score of one. I think the best one I ever had broke 23 other conkers. It was a 23. Then we had marbles. One-ers, three-ers, sixers and Japanese fivers. We would set them up in twos or threes the schoolyard and a guy would get a shot at winning your marbles by aiming at them with his marble from a distance. He might get two shots. If he didn't hit your marbles, then you won his marble.

It was great fun. If you lost a few then you would get another chance by going to another guy's stall and having a few shots at whatever marbles you wanted. They were simple times and we didn't want much. If you had a nice bike you were lucky. My bike was a Raleigh Burner. It was red with yellow tyres. Some kids got their brother's or sister's bike. Possibly a chopper or an old racer. Lucky to get it. Another thing about life in Ireland.

You ate your dinner. You ate what you got. You would be called once. You came in from the cold and ate your dinner.

Next stop is where *This Construction Life* starts at the age of 14 for me. The fun and games are over. No longer a boy. Childhood has come to a close. A man before your time. Like it or not! It is coming your way soon! *This Construction Life* is beckoning you! The index finger is calling you. It's alright, come on in!

Chapter 2

Ireland

LIFE AS AN IRISH TEENAGER GATHERS PACE!

I was a 14-year-old kid that entered the working world this summer. A new thing being a construction employee. It wasn't considered illegal to have a 14-year-old on a construction site. The construction initiation started this year. It was the summer of 1988. A beautiful summer by Irish standards. The recession of the 80s had subsided somewhat. The country modernised a lot and we were a bit better off and seemed to have a reasonably good lifestyle.

Born into a construction family in the West of Ireland was like being in the Italian mob, though. You were to eat, sleep and dream about the business. It was constant. Breakfast, dinner and tea: the site, progress and production were discussed. I was being primed at 14 years old. You are the next in line to run the family business was the message from head of the family, Jack. So, even if you didn't like it you were up. Tough if you didn't like it! You dare not mention that you didn't want to do it. If you were work-shy it wasn't going to work well for you. Lucky for me, I wanted to do it. I wanted to work on the site. I saw it as a glamorous life. I soon found out it was not! There was nothing shiny or Instagram about it! When you are hearing stuff like, no grandson of mine will be a lackey. You pups have it too easy now, was his reference to a young fellow like me. More comments like, it is the old dog for the hard road and the young pup for the footpath. I often wonder how Jack would deal with life today. The technological era. He was complaining in 1988 that we were work-shy pups. What would he say about the pups of today?

Jack was absolutely the head of the family. At 70 years of age Jack was a fearsome cigar-smoking man. He was barely 5ft 7 in height about 3ft in width and had hands like shovels and a fearsome presence of a dictator. He rarely smiled. You didn't question Jack. The men feared him, but in equal measures respected him as he himself was a tradesman. He was tough but there was an honesty and a decency to the man. By all accounts a very fast and talented tradesman in his younger days. He was a stonemason before he had success as a construction company boss. You didn't ask Jack fuck all. Jack was in charge and you were at his disposal whether you liked it or not.

Day one of the rest of my construction life. It was a beautiful summer's morning in 1988 and I hadn't even got into my second stage of sleep. I was living the dream. 14 years old, not a care in the world and just finished school for the summer holidays. I was going to be living the dream for a whole 12 weeks. A whole three months of absolute freedom, fun and hanging out with friends. Not to mention dreaming about the Californian-tanned, brown-haired bombshell gym instructor with leg warmers on the wall of my bedroom. Her boobs out and a slogan: No pain no gain. No pain, no gain saw a morning glory every morning. Not to mention the picture of Pamela Anderson on the back of the wardrobe door. She, to me, was like Duff Beer to Homer Simpson. My world was about to change dramatically in the blink of an eye. My father burst into my bedroom this particular June morning at 7am loaded with questions about what I was doing for the summer holidays. I genuinely thought it was a question. I thought I would answer by saying that I was going to play football with my friends Kevin, Brian and Dave in a local football club, along with hanging with my other friends in my locality.

Maybe even spin the bottle and get a bit of smooching in, I thought. You are not, he quipped. It was a definite no, you are not! OK, this is an order from the boss. Rubbing the sleep out of my eyes, I said, What do you mean? Get out of bed now, he ordered. Get your old jeans out and an old T-shirt and I will get you a pair of steel-toe boots. I have work for you to do! I asked, When will I be finished work as I have arranged a meeting with my friends? That's cancelled until further notice, he responded. I asked, when will I be on a break/holiday? You are on holiday when I am on holiday, he quipped which is almost never except for two weeks in August. Oh Dad... Do I have to do it? I asked as I protested. He looked annoyed and said, "Just get up." I didn't argue any further. It was decided that my future was going to be in construction. The priming had begun. I was going to take over the business after him. Like a mobster in the Sicilian mafia I was being initiated. Choices? What choices?

There were no choices. You were told and you just did what you were told. No ifs or buts. Don't ask questions, just do.

Ireland
FIRST DAY ON THE SITE...

All I can recollect was that the site was a fast-moving place. Lots of men and machinery and the noise was deafening. The dumpers and elevators were very loud. All the men looked old, in fact ancient, except the odd-20-something young bricklayer or carpenter. I would in my mind be working with them young guys. They were cool. The old men looked haggard to me. They had weather-beaten faces. Beaten by life. They were probably in their late forties to late sixties. They were able to do the work of three men by today's standards. Strong as an ox they were. Tough! They had a lot of heavy manual labour to do and they were very clever about how they organised the work. They would engineer a system of work to ensure it was productive and easier on their old bodies. They minded their jobs and they did things right. The work had to stand up to the test of time. They were as clever as engineers for men of labouring status. I was quickly whisked to the cement mixer where I got a three-minute lesson on how to mix mortar. There were three types of sand, bricklaying sand, plastering sand and sharp sand for concrete. The thing about these big, old machines was that they were heavy and cumbersome. I got a lesson on how to start the mixer first and the whole story that, if I overswung the crank while starting it, I would break my thumb. The final warning, where not to put your hand (near the drive chain) which had no guard on it! It was curtains if you put your hand in there. That meant hospital or death.

After being told how to mix mortar for the bricklayers, I absolutely fucked up the first mix as I was grappling with the fact that I couldn't lift an 8-stone bag of cement out of the cement shed, and also the fact that I had two matchstick arms without a strand of muscle in either one. Putting about 10 gallons of water in the mix didn't help. I fell into the cement bag when I tried to lift it. One old boy who was about 74 years of age entered the cement shed and told me to walk the bag to the mixer for the first few days until I felt confident to lift it. That old boy died at 94 so hard work didn't kill him.

Three days later, I was running out of the door of that same shed with an 8-stone bag on my shoulder. You would cut the cement bag in half to make it easy to put it into that mixer. The mixer was billowing out a thick blue/black diesel smoke when the load in the mixer increased. The scent of diesel smoke today still transports me back in time to those sunny days in Ireland behind the mixer. This mixer was a big, two-gauge mixer and it was about 20 years old, leaking oil and had done some time. Loads of homes were built using this mixer and there was still life in the old dog yet. Not to mention that the fuck-up came at a price. A blistering attack on me. A tirade of abuse. I guess that the old man was trying to train me to be brilliant. Good wasn't good enough. You were less inclined to fuck up again after the telling-off you got. I got it. Listen when you are being told what to do and don't cock it up. If you corrected a young fellow today in the same way he would probably call the police and have you arrested.

Five minutes into mixing the second gauge of mortar and Jack arrives on-site. He lit up a King Edward cigar and stood with a deep gaze. I was observing him while I was working the mixer. You could not miss this fellow. He had an unbelievable presence. He surveyed the site as he stood at the gate to the site. There he was in his suit and tie with a pair of suede loafers on him. His surveyor's gaze taking in every detail with that fearsome stare. A serious man. A leader. That was his character. Then he saw me behind the mixer. He walked over to me and quizzed me and then headed into the site without much chat. It was kind of a left open conversation. Like, I will be back with more questions for you later. The thing about it all was that Jack was a suited and booted businessman from a trade background. He had a tough old start and he was working on the farm from the age of about ten. He was driven and had aspirations beyond the farm. He had everything organised on-site. I remember that everything had a place on site. Production was everything. There were timber sheds, cement sheds, tool sheds and fixtures and fittings sheds for the plumbing fittings, electrical fittings and bathroom ware. It was a very organised and clean site. No waste and definitely no rubbish strewn all around the site. The man cared about what he did. He was diligent. There was an honesty about him, although he was tough. The houses had to be built well. No room for poor workmanship on our sites. Everything had to be done exceptionally. Precision and durability were very important. Solid homes better built by us.

I was kind of hooked on construction after a few hard weeks. I liked it. I better make a bigger effort! A few weeks later they were leaving me in charge of deliveries, answering telephones, ordering materials and signing for materials, and an introduction to sales of housing stock on Sundays between 2pm and 6pm. At 14 you don't expect to be given such responsibility. I was enjoying it and maybe that enthusiasm was noted. I believed in the brand and thought that we were the best at what we did. We were the best at what we did! Those homes stand today like they were built yesterday. I have no doubt now looking back. Hence the Rolls-Royce name we had. We had high standards and we were possibly a little bit confident in ourselves. But hey, you know what they say. Black Cat – Black Kitten. Jack believed it, so I believed it. I was getting £40 for a 40-hour week and I was the richest teenager at the seaside at the weekends. I would go to the seaside with my father on Saturday afternoon after work. My mother would take the younger kids there earlier in the summer for about a month of the school holiday.

Sunday was a rest day. We went to Mass. We had to. Yes, I did go to Mass on Sunday because it was a mortal sin for you not to turn up to church on Sunday. The neighbours would be tut-tutting if you left five minutes before the end. Six Hail Marys and four Our Fathers if you confessed at confession that you didn't go to Mass on Sunday. That was the culture. Let us leave that one for another day! I was the richest teenager of my age at the seaside. I had £40 of a wage a week. I probably worked 60 hours.

I was ordered by the old man to hand up £20 to my mother. She did a trade-off with me. I could keep the £20 but I had to do a job for her. I was to clean the house in her absence. A good deal. I was by far the richest kid in town at 14. My friends might be lucky enough to get a fiver each for the week.

The £40 wage packet went far. Very far. I could buy an Ice cream cone for 30 pence and candyfloss for 20 pence. Two of each was £1. A pint of rock shandy in the pub, which was a mixture of fizzy club lemon and fizzy club orange mixed in a pint glass, was £1. I could buy myself and my friend two each and we were still only at a fiver. Pole position, a Formula One racing game was 10p a game. Ten games over two days and now we are at £6. Bumper cars were 20p a ride. Five goes and we are at £7. I usually had £32 or £33 to bank on a Sunday night. I used the next £40 on the next weekend. The next Sunday that £32 was banked. Jack gave me my first wallet. He said always have money in your wallet. If your wallet had money in it then it will attract more. The thought of money brings more of the same. What a great philosophy. I always keep a £50 note in my wallet now.

These were happy times. We had no mobile phones, no internet and not many computers. The bank teller to deposit your money in the bank. People discussed matters with each other.

In the pub the air was blue from cigarette smoke. This had one great advantage. No smell of farts! The only downside to being in a cigarette smoke-filled pub was that it made your eyes itch and you would be coughing your guts up the next day! But otherwise all good. That summer I learned lots of new things on the site. Making concrete window sills and lintels, mixing mortar, placing concrete, piling foundations, steel fixing, concreting ground beams, loading and unloading trucks, driving machinery, loading roofs, erecting scaffolding, being a carpenter's mate, tending bricklayers and plasterers. I learned a hell of a lot about good housekeeping, storing materials and how to construct a house. It was a brilliant time. I also learned a bit about things my mother wouldn't like to hear. I became a man overnight. Construction boys can be colourful with their language, to say the least!

The best of all was the fact that I learned how to work with old machinery. I also learned how to fix it. We knew almost instantly what was wrong when it broke down. We had so many tools to fix machines that time on the site. We supplied all the construction tools to our own men. We had a tool shelf in the main office. All the tools were cleaned and returned to that spot every evening. Shovels were cleaned and left in the oils and lubricants shed in the evening. That shed was in the compound where the mixer, cement shed and timber sheds were situated. The men used to put notches on their shovel to mark their one. If a fellow tried to take your shovel, well, then there was going to be words. I saw a big bust-up between two grown men once. I will never see one again. No one will fight you over a shovel today. They won't even use the damn things.

Basically, we knew a lot about the machines we were using. They were like an extension of your arm. There was a connection between you and them. Knowing what we know today about the universe, it is not far out to think of that connection between man and all the matter on this planet. We also knew beforehand what not to do. The thought was out there so we were getting the vibe back, like a signal. Things like do not put a mortar bucket on a particular flap of the elevator that was damaged or the bucket would fall off. We also knew that the belt would jump now and then and you would be able to time it so you could eliminate a breakdown or the destruction of materials. Being tuned in was a must. If you were not copped on or tuned in, well, you would get hurt.

Health and safety standards were a bit loose. There was an unwritten code that men knew to be careful. When lifting heavy materials, you were told to take care of your work colleague first. His fingers were more important than your own fingers. Care for your fellow workers' welfare was important. There were very few accidents. If something was heavy and you were struggling you would still hold onto the object, as dropping it was not an option. This gave you a steely determination. A new fellow who started work on our site would be a challenge for him! The men would tell you if he was a liability. He would have to be warned if he started doing things on site that endangered himself or anyone else. If he was or foostering or dropping heavy items or hurting other men by just not being careful enough. He would get one warning. A dismissal if he did something stupid a second time. Most of the time the individual knew himself and would just leave. No second chances. Eliminate the risk immediately. Today it would be a case of the problem is between the keyboard and the chair. In that particular era the problem was on-site. Get him out of here. A case of leave your feelings at home!

This Construction Life

While I sit here in a fabulous public library in Santa Clara, California, I can't help but notice the enthusiasm of two young kids in the park with their mother drawing with chalk on the tarmac of a park footpath outside the window. They are drawing like they never drew before. It reminds me of that enthusiasm that I had as that 14-year-old kid. Work like the money does not matter. The old men on the site used to smile at me possibly because I brought this amazing energy to the site. Blond-haired kid with a free mind. No hang-ups, no bills and definitely no worries. The age of innocence! Spiritually, mentally and emotionally you should be free. Free from fear, free from worry. Get up every day with a smile and the attitude that I am going to smash it today. Another day of fun is on its way. A good way to start is with gratitude. Be grateful for just being here. Be grateful for being able to get up and go free of any incumbrance. This leads me to where fear crept up on me. A situation occurred that you could only call a shock to the system...

Ireland
LIFE AS AN IRISH TEENAGER! EXPOSURE TO A
NEW WORLD

*Jack and the deputy Sheriff ... Lesson 1. In the event of an
emergency, act fast!*
The grandfather was a knowledgeable chap. He was a leader.
Men looked up to this guy. I did, too. He had a lot of wisdom
and the will and the heart of a Lion, or so it seemed. I never got
to that stage of having a close and personal chat with him. You
would not get into his space or his mind. He was very private.
The lion came out the day the deputy sheriff arrived on-site.

It was another of those boiling summer's days in Ireland.
They are rare enough. It was July 1989. We were preparing to
hand over two semi-detached houses to clients on Friday. It
was Thursday and there were tradesmen everywhere on this
corner of the site. The labourers were cleaning everything. The
painters were completing the last few jobs. The plumbers and
electricians were commissioning their work. The grandfather
was directing operations. Everyone was working hard.

Out of the blue this Isuzu Trooper SUV appeared at speed
in convoy with two Toyota Camry cars. They pulled up
outside these two houses where all the men were working.
This big fellow (deputy sheriff), about 6' 8" in height, and a
cop nearly as tall got out of the SUV at speed. The big fellow
started shouting, who is in charge here?! My grandfather, being
sarcastic, asked, who is asking? The deputy sheriff continued
shouting while reading aloud a writ saying I am here to collect

an unpaid debt to the Revenue Commissioners of £500. I am requesting immediate payment today or I will proceed to seize assets. My grandfather responded that the money was paid two weeks earlier. Proven records exist. Remember this is the 80s in Ireland. It was a decade marred with recession. Truthfully the money had been paid. The Revenue were coming down on businesses to try to get every last drop of blood! I mean every last penny you had. Killing businesses was their business.

The sheriff ordered the two toothless bailiffs that had emerged from the other cars to seize everything and started using heavy-handed rhetoric. Talk of cameras recording this site. The owners being exposed and threats of ruining reputations. Really unnecessary behaviour. This is the point where my grandfather lost his temper. He never lost his temper in front of me. He basically started going at this fellow like a Rottweiler.

He told him to gather up his toothless crew and get the f**k off his site or he would have him arrested for trespass and intimidation. Cut to the next scene! The deputy who was about 30 started pushing the grandfather. The guard stepped in between them as they squared up to each other. Now my grandfather was a man with fierce presence but only 5' 7". Only he ruled in this environment and no pup was going to order him around. Not this, as he would say, upstart. The grandfather stepped back then and coolly took off this trench coat and laid it over the finished steel railing. This is the point when I was calculating this is going to get messy. Then he started to roll up his sleeves slowly. His hands were half the length of his arm.

While rolling the sleeves all he was saying was, The last fellow I belted didn't get up for a long time and that was a long time ago. Jack then went for this fellow. He kind of made a swipe of a cut in a boxing fashion at the deputy again as if to belt him. This young fella hit him first. David and Goliath were gnashing and gnarling and generally being pretty mean to each other.

Jack and the deputy sheriff – thinking time!

The cop stood between them. In true Irish fashion the cop said, Now, now, lads. Let's not be getting carried away… That was some help! I remember the cop really struggling to keep them at bay. Like a schoolteacher keeping two terriers in a schoolyard at arm's length from each other. The cop had less power (a lower rank) than this feckin idiot of a deputy sheriff. He was there only to uphold the peace. In the interim a skirmish was breaking out between the bailiffs and the labourers when the bailiffs in a heavy-handed manor turned off machinery and tried to take control of them. Our labouring men, old as they were, closed them off. There were more of us than them. A very poor way of asking to collect £500.

I was stressed, to say the least. My eyes were moving in my head like the ball of a pinball machine. I ran to the site office and called my dad who was in our city office. He answered. I was panicking with words. Dad! Dad! Come quick, the sheriff is here and him and grandad are going to start fighting. It is serious. Grandad had his sleeves rolled up. Come quick. Can you imagine a telephone call like that? Your seventy-year-old father was ready to go boxing a state employee. He told me go out and tell the sheriff that he would return in ten minutes and he would sort it out.

Out I run from the site office shouting above the noise of the argument in my adolescent voice. Wait, wait, I spoke to my father and he said he will be here in a few minutes and he will sort it all out. Please wait....The cop let me tell him what my father said. He cooled the two dogs down and said, wait for the man to come. The cop was now correcting the younger deputy sheriff, using the bit of gumption he had. A stern look and an erect index finger. 'You are on the edge' sort of gesture.

I think that Grandad was relieved that the fight was over, to be honest. His fighting days were over. The old boy was an adolescent returning to his youth. Once a man, twice a boy, they say. My dad came to the site and sorted it out. There were two groups hanging around. The sheriff and his crew and then our crew. I have to hand it to Jack. He gave that punk a run for his money. I am sure the punk was observing the size of the grandfather's hands when the grandfather was going for him. Jesus, what was this young pup thinking pushing Jack? Nobody would even dream of riling him.

That was a great bit of entertainment which calmed the day down. There were fellows in different parts of that site that day talking about the incident and Jack. Arms and legs were going to be added to this story. This big fella was a pig, to be honest. He was still threatening as he was leaving in his SUV that this wasn't the end of it. The grandfather was hitting back: You are right, this is far from the end. I will see to it that you will get your arse reddened for this behaviour. Blackened with a hurley in fact. You met your match here. The father was telling my grandfather to stop. If I am being honest it was kind of a comical sketch playing out before my eyes. Not one I would like to see repeated. Irish people are the funniest people in the world until you fight with them. The word 'intensity' comes to mind. If you are Irish and have the following traits of being intensely nice, intensely friendly and intensely funny – well, then you are going to be intensely in a rage when the sheriff starts throwing his weight around and making false demands. That was a scene I will never forget till the day I am dust.

Ireland
LIFE AS AN IRISH TEENAGER!

The site, the young carpenter and the girl next door
That summer passed and on the next housing project it was the summer of 1990. I was a carpenter's mate this summer. I had to learn each trade this summer. Having a hammer and a carpenter's belt were my tools. I fought for a rise in my wages. £60 a week was agreed. I was going to be putting in 80 hours a week if my old man had his way. He was another sort of sheriff. From joisting houses to installing flooring to roofing. I did it all this summer. One day the carpenter asked me to get a 25kg box of 4" wire nails from the sheds. I noticed the site looked quiet when I was in the shed. On my return he asked me to walk down between the roof trusses and look back along the truss and tell him if the roof truss was plumb. I thought that this is a bit weird. I asked, why are you asking me? You know

the answer to this yourself. You have a good eye and you know already. What's this about!

He told me, shut up and go on. So, off I trotted down between the trusses to the back elevation of the house. I was then facing him. Well, is it straight? I was looking. Yeah, I responded, it's straight. Are you sure? he said. He was gesturing to me to look behind me. I hadn't a clue what he was talking about. I walked towards the front elevation. When I got close to him, he whispered, "Look into the garden of the houses behind." I returned to the same spot and did just that, only to observe a young girl about 18 absolutely starkers on a sun lounger taking in the rays. Her pert little boobies facing the sun. She didn't seem to have any hang-ups at all. No body shame! Why would she!? She looked like a new Rolls-Royce.

Then I looked below the scaffold. Half the feckin workforce were pretending to be doing something in the gardens of these houses that backed onto the house of the young lady. My old man was probably gone off-site and the boys knew he wasn't around. Jack was probably down a trench ordering some older fellows (by that I mean the over-seventies) to put in a main sewer or something. There were painters painting the wrong elevation of the next pair of semi-detached houses. They should have been somewhere else. Very adolescent. But that's boys, is it not?! Below me, two young plasterers leaning on the scaffold guard rail smoking cigarettes and drooling. That was a change for them two brothers. They would fight over a pint of milk. I mean roll-around-the-floor fights. They were good at the plastering but would fight like Noel and Liam Gallagher from Oasis. I can't say I ever saw a construction-related situation again that involved a naked lady showing her assets so blatantly. Her parents must have been at work. The girl knew exactly what she was doing! Being a teenager that year was full of emotion and excitement. We hadn't any technology and we were happy with our lot. No one was trying to tell us we needed to be someone else or we needed to have a pair of Nike trainers that were £150. You did want certain things and then you would have to save for them. No kid ever expected anything different. Had enough!

The dumper accident, my father and the dip in the stream: 1991

My old man decided to buy another second-hand dumper. We were down to two dumpers from the original four 1960s set. They were now about 30 years old. Thwaites Dumpers. Made in England. Check them out on the internet. They went on forever. The parts were almost obsolete because of their age. But in true Irish style we kept fixing them UNTIL THERE WAS NO LIFE LEFT. We needed to improve on our ageing plant. My old man in his wisdom decided to buy a left-hand drive dumper because it was value for money. He would always be looking for a deal.

It was a fine Saturday morning in May and we were ready to fill an open space with topsoil. We would be waking up the new residents of this spanky new neighbourhood. My old man took one of the original dumpers and gave me the new one. The new dumper was mine to joyride, or so I thought. The digger driver was filling the dumpers with topsoil for us. The topsoil was situated near a stream. We in turn were doing the run in the dumpers to a new green area. Dumping the topsoil in neat heaps and returning for the next load. My dumper was filled first. I took off. It was a highly powered nippy dumper, although the steering seemed a bit odd. I, like any teenager, took off like a bat out of hell when I got this yoke on the main road. It was a form of legal joyriding. The feeling of freedom and the wind in your hair and not a care in the world. It was fantastic! A legal non-substance high. OK, maybe a diesel fumes high. We owned the land so it wasn't yet a public highway. Legal? Maybe.

Then there were a few bends on the way to the spoil drop-off point. When I came to the first bend in the road, I turned the steering wheel. Nothing happened. I turned the wheel more and then it did a 180 back on itself. I immediately tried to right the dumper before crashing over some road kerbs and then oversteering the opposite direction and then barely missed a new, out of the box blue Alfa Romeo car before I got it on the straight. I then floored it. Pedal to the metal. Unfortunately for me my father, who was coming behind me, saw everything. When I reached the drop-off area he went mental. He ordered me to take his dumper and gave me a right old bollocking.

I took his dumper, dumped off the load of topsoil and made my way back to the spoil heap down beside this stream. When I turned the corner to head down the incline, I could see smoke coming out of the stream. The dumper was hidden by reeds. It was in the stream on its side, the engine still billowing out exhaust fumes. My old fella was on the far bank of the stream wet through, like a sewer rat. He roared, "Don't say a word!" I didn't. But I have to admit I laughed a lot, as did the digger driver. We pulled it out with the JCB. There were no accident report forms filled in either. It was just get the damn thing out of there. The old man was so covered in muck and slurry he had to go home to change his clothes. He was absolutely drenched. Bet he was sorry he took the new jalopy off me. I had the work finished by the time he returned to site.

In the end we had to get rid of this old dumper. A few other things happened. It took off on its own one day. The handbrake was up and it was idling. Then out of nowhere it started to head away on its own. Either we had a ghost on-site or it was part of the dumper! The men maintained that it was possessed. Weird! When the workforce refused to drive it after that incident it had to go. The dumper was sold on swiftly after that for a small sum to a guy on-site who knew he could fix the steering problem with it. Personally, I just think there was more going on. You never felt in control of it. I am sure it is now rusting away safely in a graveyard in County Clare.

Chapter 3

Ireland

BEFORE SEPTEMBER COMES 1991

Back to the summer madness! My Cousin Vinny and disco lessons.

It is coming close to September again. School is looming. What a blast I had during the summer on the sites. A few pounds banked, not to mention the girls I was chasing and the friends I was meeting at the seaside. The last 12 weekends were great. I didn't know how good I had it. I was still a bit shy around girls. One weekend I decided to tag along to this disco with my cousin who, might I add, was a bit of a tearaway. He loved devilment ever since he was an infant. The first incident I saw him get up to devilment was when he was five and I was four. He picked up a sizable rock in his garden and handed it to me. He proceeded to tell me to throw it through the window of the shed. I wouldn't do it as his mother was watching out the kitchen window. He pulled the rock out of my hand in temper and then threw it at speed through the window. BOSH! He paid for that one. His mother reddened his arse for the offence. Rightly so! It was his sixth time doing it.

By now a rebellious teenager. He was a great guy. He always included me whenever I wanted to go with him anywhere. He was into punk music and he was the exact opposite to me. I was listening to Aha and he was listening to the Sex Pistols. His hair was dyed in a purple mohawk and he wore 16-hole red Doc Martens boots with a chain hanging from his torn jeans. He was a real punk! Johnny Rotten would be proud.

This one Saturday night we were at this aptly named disco called the "Atlantic" which happened to be beside the Atlantic Ocean. The next stop New York, 3000 miles west. The cousin decided to take me under his wing. He said I will show you how to ask a girl to dance at the disco. You can hang with us. The cousin walks out on the dance floor in front of me and starts throwing shapes and a cock-of-the-walk stroll. He was a popular guy and full of confidence. For me, a shy guy, this was a great education! I knew that he was going to do something funny. I hung back a few metres from him and observed. What I witnessed wouldn't win him a medal for political correctness today. The girls were snotty but then they probably knew him. It went like this!

Cousin: Do you want to dance?

Response from girl 1: No!

Cousin: Ah sorry, I didn't see the wooden leg there. HA!

Cousin to girl 2: Da you want to dance?

Girl 2: After the way you spoke to her, definitely no way!

Cousin: Did you stick the freckles on before you came out or, are they permanent?

By girl 10 and after a fair few slaps, girl 10 says yes. The cousin and the girl are walking to the dance floor and he turns to me and says, Nine times out of ten there is always a chance. The guy knew the secret to life. The guy was hilarious. He had me up to all sorts of mischief like knocking on somebody's front door and running away. Then repeating the act just to drive the homeowner up the wall. The homeowner would be ranting about calling the guards. The cousin used to say the guards will never come. Who would leave the comfort of their own home in a small town like this to a call out of a game called "Knock a Dolly". I was an amateur at this game and almost got caught a few times. This made the little fucker more eager to get me caught.

Ireland
WHEN SEPTEMBER COMES.... SCHOOL ! 1991

I have to bring an all-boys' school into the mix as it paints a picture of life as a teenager in Ireland in the late 1980s and early 1990s. School, site and then school again. School was like a batter fest for a week when we would get back after the holidays. All that testosterone. It was beatings for the first three days again for the first years. Head first into dustbins. Lads getting their heads flushed down toilets. Wedgies! If no one knows what a wedgie is, well, it is something to do with ripped underpants and broken testicles! This only happened to me in the first year. I was a bit unhinged after I got a few beatings in the first year. You learn how to function quick. You had to be quick and cruel to survive. If some lad wanted to be

43

a smart-arse and have a go at me. Well, then, I made sure he would get hurt. I made sure that I would drop a desk on his foot during the struggle and then floor him with a knee in the balls. A fellow wouldn't be that keen to beat me again. Hesitant would be a good word. Most fellows stayed away from me in that respect.

Little, the half of a duo called "Little and Large", two punks in my class, learned that one the hard way. I broke Little's wrist in a bust-up. The bollix deserved it. He beat a poor, defenceless weak guy in our class to a pulp for absolutely no reason. I intervened and he thought he would do the same to me. He found out the hard way! Arm in a sling for six weeks hard way. He didn't bank on meeting muscles from the site.

Lads would be beating each other, catching each other in headlocks and unleashing slicers as we used to call them, with and 18-inch ruler. This used to happen when the teacher would ask someone to stand up and read some paragraph or answer some homework question. The guy would stand up from his seat and proceed to read or answer the teacher. The guy behind would be charged with unleashing the punishment. They guy behind would carefully remove an 18-inch ruler and start to get the ruler in position without the teacher noticing. Then he would raise the ruler just above backside of the guy in front of him. He would then drop it at guillotine speed and slice like he was slicing thin slices of ham. The offender would cough at the same time. The victim would squelch out a screaming sound while rubbing his arse and everyone would burst their sides laughing. The teacher would then go into a tirade of shouting,

"What's going on down there?" The offender would get a telling-off but he would be still laughing all the way through and this would create even more angst for the teacher. The victim of the slicing might knock all the stuff off the offender's desk out of rage. Then the teacher would turn on him. Hilarious stuff. This would knock at least five minutes off the class. If the class was boring, well, it might happen five times. It would usually happen in a lady called Hynes's class. They called her Nana because of her age. Bastards! This reminds me of the story of the Irish teachers we had as temps. ***Tinker Bell and The Green Giant!***

Chapter 4

Ireland

WHEN SEPTEMBER COMES: BOYS WILL BE BOYS.

Tinker Bell and The Green Giant.

We had an Irish teacher in the fourth year of secondary school who was ready to pop and going on maternity leave. She was a tough cookie and by all accounts she was not missed by some real comedians in our class. She was very strict about us learning Irish. She was an able woman. She needed to be. She was replaced by a young girl, nicknamed Tinker Bell. The guys in my class called her that because she had red, long, curly hair. The boys would reference her as a member of the travelling community. She was an attractive 23-year-old, softly spoken young woman and wanted to teach us. These lads that I shared a class with wanted her out, on the instructions of the two pups. Little and Large, we shall call them for privacy reasons.

The class would start and she would then turn to the blackboard and start to write. A tennis ball would hit the board at speed missing her face by millimetres. The ball would bounce down the class. Little and Large had primed everyone to go with the flow. If the ball landed near you put it in your schoolbag. Then pass it back to the offender. She would lose her temper and then start screaming. On the second day, she called in the principal. He came to the class and all looked calm. He would threaten us with expulsion for those **two** responsible. He knew who the culprits were. She left after one week teaching us. I didn't like what these guys were doing. It was harder, though, to go up against them as a duo. It meant a black eye or maybe a broken rib.

The next lady arrived. She was about 4' 6" in height, had a squeaky voice and wore this **pea-green jumper,** hence the name Green Giant. A cruel bunch of bastards. Again, the same tactics started. Tennis-balling the blackboard at a fast pace and more. She called the principal. He visited again. Another warning. This particular morning the duo decided to up the punishment level a notch. Young fellas in Ireland can be a right cruel bunch when they get an idea into their heads.

They instructed everyone in the class to turn their desks and chairs to face the back of the class. I protested and had a real fucking face-off with these two pups. Head-butting and real aggression. But I gave in for peace of mind. They rolled the blackboard into the corner of the room. The Green Giant arrived and she started screaming at us to, "Turn your desks and chairs and face the front of the room." No one moved or looked up from their books. She lost it and called the principal. He arrived as we suspected he would and we were all reading our books, facing the right way and the blackboard and teacher's desk were in the correct position. She left the next day. Then we had no teacher or so we thought...

The real retribution was yet to come. For every reaction there is an equal but opposite reaction. It was not over for Little and Large yet! Their punishment was yet to come.

A week later we had him, the principal, for Irish. Not funny anymore! He used to randomly pick people for punishment. Those two little feckers wished to have no Irish class but instead they got the principal himself. The fact that he had to take our class was a pain in the arse for him. He had other things to do. He decided: I am going to make these two little feckers pay.

I will tell you what he used to do and how he used to do it. Little and Large used to start misbehaving between classes and then the principal would arrive for class and say, Ahem, right then. Let's do the bags, lads! Everyone in the class would throw their school bags to one aisle in the room. Then the boys beside the isle would stack them in several piles as high as they could. There were lunch boxes and hurleys included. Then the principal would call little or large out to the aisle. Then little out of the duo would be asking for mercy and things like please sir no, not again. Talk about wimping out!

Teacher would start telling him why he was called out. Then he would catch him by his sideburn and walk him to the first mountain of bags. Then he would make him walk up the bags and on his way down the principal would hold his hand at the high point thus tearing at your little sideburn of hair. Everyone used to remotely feel the pain. But we were entertained. Little or Large would be screeching with pain. That was only the first bag. There were five more to go. There was an uncontrollable amount of laughing in the class. Little and Large more than paid the price that year. The fun was over for them and the fun was only beginning for us. I'd say that Tinker Bell and the Green Giant got more revenge out of these pups in their absence. Laughable.

The great thing about my school in Ireland was that they promoted sports of all influence. You got a pass on some mischief from the principal if you played rugby or hurling. I started playing rugby and absolutely loved the sport. For six years in secondary school I played rugby and enjoyed every moment of it. I would say that I was as fit as a fiddle and ribbed and, to top that, harder than a coffin nail. I loved tackling people. It was a badge of honour for me, a nine-stone lad to take down a 24-stone fellow. They hated to see me coming to tackle them. I used to run at the guy during training and run at speed and hit them in the shins with my boney shoulders. The whack of that used to be enough to drop them. I think the worst injury I got was a broken nose. I got off light. I also played for Garryowen Rugby Club as a flanker. Fighting for my position with a guy called Dave Brown was the norm. We didn't like each other much. I suppose I was his biggest rival and he mine. A few rough remarks now and then. There was a lot of sportsman respect too!

I was a slight lad, with a body full of muscle. I had to make a mark because I was a small lad in comparison to some of these guys. They nicknamed me the Psycho in the end. I used to get the crash balls. I used to go in low. This stood to me as I never got an injury. Don't know how many I injured, though. I would say a lot. My fellow rugby players had black and blue shins, I suspect!

Ireland

WHEN SEPTEMBER COMES: BOYS WILL BE BOYS.
MORE SCHOOL DEVILMENT BEFORE HEADING
BACK TO SITE FOR ANOTHER SUMMER

Little and Large, Mr C and the "Dick" drawing. They didn't learn!

Little and Large were always fuelling each other in devilment. One particular sunny Friday afternoon we were in the physics lab. To be honest, it was hard to focus on a sunny May day. The sun peering through the window. I suppose this is where Little and Large fell down. The teacher was doing the theory part for a physics experiment on the blackboard. It was boring. The duo decided to draw an animated picture of the teacher with a dick coming out of his forehead. One fellow would start the drawing. The other would then take over and then draw the next part, and so on. They took turns drawing this animated drawing of Mr C. They were, however, unaware that he had twigged it. The class noticed he had noticed them. They didn't. They were seated just below the teacher's podium desk. They were crouched down in a hiding position.

The teacher, Mr C, pounced on them. He ripped the picture out of their hands and said, Hmmm… what have we here now? Very interesting, as he stroked his beard. It was a picture of him and his beard, his small mouth and this big manhood coming out of his forehead. We knew it wasn't going to end well for the duo. He showed it to the class. We laughed collectively for what seemed an age. Then Mr C announced that Mr L and Mrs L would like to share their artistic views with the class. He said to Large, You brought the girlfriend, I see. He ordered the two of them to come up onto the podium and draw this wonderful piece of art on the blackboard. He rubbed out the theorem off the blackboard. They were apologising and squirming for forgiveness. They were pleading, No, no, Sir, we are sorry. It won't happen again.

Mr C handed one of them a new, long piece of chalk and said, Draw. This is an interesting experiment, isn't it, lads? he quipped as he folded his arms in a serious manner and nodded like a cartoon character. Sarcasm is the lowest form of wit. We knew there was a reckoning coming. He still had the metre stick still in one hand. Now hand the chalk to your girlfriend, he said to Large. Get her to do the next part of the masterpiece. Our suspense was building. Not only have we a Michelangelo but we have his girlfriend, too, he joked. They two bollixes hated the joke. We were waiting and the suspense was building. All the time they were drawing, they waited for the fallout. Mr C then moved in just as they were getting to the point of drawing the willy part, and he started to leather them into a corner with a metre stick. It was priceless. We laughed our nuts off. It was entertainment like no other. He kettled the two of them into a corner and beat the daylights out of them.

It was pure entertainment as they usually intimidated everyone else. He didn't suspend them or anything. It was a better way of resolving a problem for him. Mr C was saving himself the rigmarole of a procedure of putting them on report for a month. This is a procedure where the parents would have to sign off on their homework for a month. This would involve meetings and the like. Too much hassle for Mr C. They wouldn't complain him as it would spell more pain for them. Parents would have to get involved. Pain at home as well as school. Possibly being grounded for a month etc… I think that went well, lads, Mr C quipped as he marched the two fools back to their seats.

That was that: situation resolved. He had no further hassle from the two. They were humiliated but free of any further incumbrance. The few slaps were the lesser of the two evils. They would never learn, though. They received many more from other teachers as they just couldn't contain their devilment. They had a small bit of power, too. Prime characteristics of a future banker! They used to intimidate others where they could. This earned them what you might call street cred. So, when they got a public beating like that, no one felt sorry for them.

Ireland
SUMMER HOLIDAYS!

My Friend John. On the site!
On a Friday night when I was about 17 years old the mother would let me have her car. I would be gone. Out of the door like a rocket. Over to my friend John's house to collect him and head into the city to spot some girls. This fellow was a real character. His mother used to be very vocal with him. She knew he was a bit of a pup. He used to get a tenner from his father on the QUIET. His father was an inoffensive, calm guy. His father would say to him, Don't tell your mother I gave you money. The mother would be giving John the third degree about being home at 11 o'clock at the latest. He'd say, OK, Mum, no problem, now stop hassling me. Then he would close the door in the hall on the way out and say to me, My father is my mother's bitch but I will never be her bitch. He used to say, No problem, Jackie, to his mother.

He was a lunatic. I would be driving the car into town and he would out of the blue say to me pull up quick, I feel sick. Right here beside these people. I would pull in next to a couple. He would proceed to roll down the window of the car. Note I say 'roll down' the window. No electric windows then. He would put on an Australian accent and address the people on the footpath. Excuse me, excuse me, where is a place called Lahinch? he would ask in his Aussie twang. Lahinch is a seaside town. He would say, I hear the surf is great out there! The people on the pavement would go through the directions.

He would copy them on every part of it AND FOUL UP WHAT THEY WERE SAYING. When that would be finished he would say, Feck off, you tools, in his own accent and say, That's the worst directions I ever got in my life. Then he would roll up the window and tell me to drive! We would repeat it a few times going around the city. Great entertainment.

John thought, like me, that the site was a glamorous place to work. He was always pestering me for a summer job on the site. I was always trying to put him off working with us. He was a bit soft for us, or so I thought. I thought the construction business would not suit him and Jack would be all over him like a rash, critiquing his work. This will not be pretty. So, my answer was no! You don't want to work with us. Go and get a job at the petrol station. This guy wouldn't give up. He kept annoying me for a job in our firm. Eventually he cornered my old man at home one Friday after school. My old man tried his best to talk him out of it. He persisted. My old man gave him a job and said, "Don't be afraid to say it's not for you."

On his first day, I was busy working at the mixer, mixing mortar for the bricklayers when I saw Jack talking to my friend. I was behind Jack. My friend was busily painting a side gate to a house and Jack thought he would correct him on his work. The only problem was my friend had these big headphones on his head and a Walkman cassette recorder with the volume up to the last. He clearly couldn't hear or see Jack. I saw this pending situation from a distance beginning to unfold. I made my way to the scene to fend off the offensive. I was on my way when I saw Jack put his hand behind the headphone and pull them off

John's head. So, one minute it was Guns N' Roses belting out paradise city and then it was this 70-year-old man shouting at you. You can't be listening to music on this job, he roared at this young fellow. You can listen to music at 5 o'clock when you are finished WORK! My friend was so innocent that he started saying that it made him happy and he was more likely to do a better job with the music. Jack said, You must be joking. This is a building site, not Butlin's.

Ireland
MY FRIEND JOHN

At this point I was standing behind Jack, miming to my friend to shut up. I was doing a 'cut throat' sign with my hand. Shut up! The fecker was still not getting it. He kept trying to argue his point. Then I intervened and said, It's alright, Jack, I will explain to him. I eventually got it into his thick skull to shut his gob. The old boy went away not before he laid some more ground rules. No music, ten minutes for tea break and a half-hour for lunch. No talking or lackeying, got it! Friend: Yes, Sir Mr President Sir, and he saluted him like an Army officer. The old boy was disgusted. He just walked away, shaking his head. A dinosaur. I clipped John on the ear. Do you want a job or not?! He is not your mother's bitch, I barked. Twit! Wanker, he responded. Then we were flipping each other off with the middle finger. Three days into the job my dad asked him, How is the job going? He said, You know what, you and Pat are OK, but Jack is a complete bollix. He is an old git! A killjoy! There is something seriously wrong with Jack, he joked sarcastically. Both myself and my old man laughed to the point of being physically sick. We asked was it only now that he was coming to that conclusion. He did six weeks and said he was going to take the final six weeks as holiday.

One Monday he came in and announced that he was off on Friday! He could take a break; I, on the other hand, wasn't allowed. He needed a break from Jack. Possibly, Jack needed a break from him. When he was gone, Jack was enquiring, where is that young pup? He was actually OK. I thought Jaysus, Jack has a heart. That's the thing about tough businessmen. They are sometimes hard heads. It takes a lot of digging to find their human side. When you do it only lasts a while. Jack was a committed soul. Completely committed to construction. You always need a hobby. His hobby was construction, too. The bank managers had a hard time controlling him during poor, economic times. During hard times the guy kept spending money on getting as many pile foundations in and houses built as he could. It was a cheaper time to do it with high unemployment. The guy said, we will never get the work done as cheap again. Looking back on it, he was so right.

THE WORRIED BANK MANAGER, A MILLION QUID AND NON-CONVENTIONAL JACK

One day the bank manager did come to site. Hilarious scene! Jack, the bold boy. Non-conformance being Jack's goal. No one was going to tell this old boy what to do! Not even the priest or the Pope for that matter. The bank manager came looking for him one day. At this point in time he owed the bank a million quid and was building at a rate of knots while most contractors were going bust. He was going to build his way out of the recession. It paid off. At the time the bank manager came to the site. He was shitting bricks and Jack was building like it was going out of fashion. The bank manager was probably going to be fired. The s**t always flows downhill in the bank and then it flows onto the borrower. Not so!

The day the young bank manager and his assistant arrived to the site, Jack walked down to the wettest, dirtiest part of the site. The bank manager couldn't go down to meet him. The manager and his assistant were loudly asking him to return up to dry ground so they could have a chat with him. He responded that he didn't want to talk to them. He said I have nothing to say to you. I know why you are here and the answer is no! You two have no clue about economics or life. Houses will sell if not today then tomorrow. A good house will hold its value always. I will not stop. Now if you have no more to ask me then I bid you good day. I am busy. Tough nut. Today the bank would foreclose on you. I would say that he would have gone cracked if they even harboured an idea of doing such a thing. Lots of things might get broken, including their necks. It was a good thing that these two feared him. He told me that those two apes want to kill the momentum we have here. They see houses, I see all the money we are going to make and the timeless product we are going to sell. We have three times in collateral to what I owe. Jack used to say to me, always be in a position to tell the banks to fuck off. How right he was about that one. I found that out the hard way afterwards. For years later I worked diligently and cautiously made assessments only to find that I hadn't made enough safety provisions. Jack was a bright man and maybe I should have planned things better. The lack of grey hair probably contributed to that one. Read on to find out more.

Chapter 5

This Construction Life.

THE ACCIDENTAL EMIGRANT! IRELAND

The Great Recession

Fast-forward 15 years. Life can change in a split second. We had arrived at that dreaded day. The day nobody wanted to ever see. Everything was about to go tits up globally! The financial industry blew up and went into meltdown. It was all over the news that the American stock market was crashing and the share values were dropping like a stone. I was listening to the news on my car radio during my lunch break in Ireland while taking a few minutes in out of the rain. It was July 2007. At night on TV there were pictures on the news of big corporate giants of world banks that were in major financial difficulty and could collapse. Banks collapsing! I thought, this is serious. American banks collapsing! Not even a remote possibility? I had an idea that this would mean some belt tightening for us in Ireland, too! I totally underestimated the size of the fallout or the impact it would have on me, a construction man, and many others like me. Honestly, I think everyone has forgotten this economic meltdown. Let's hope we never see one again.

Hold that thought and rewind a few years before. The catalyst was the early noughties. Just a year after the dust settled post-2001 terror attacks in America. The global markets had recovered very quickly and things were heating up economically worldwide. In Ireland the euro currency had been adopted and land values went from hundreds of thousands to millions between 2002 and 2003. The federalists in Europe were busy trying to consolidate the European Union, i.e. take control. The euro currency really hurt Ireland. It spurned high inflation in Ireland. Things became very expensive! Both my father and I were conservative, old-school building contractors. Jack taught us. We knew the value of everything in our business. This is the tipping point where things were beginning to get out of hand. The jump in value of everything was huge. Rounding up the pound to the euro eventually took the cost of £1 = €1.27 advised by the EU to £1 = €2. Ireland was in better shape than Italy. Italy still hasn't really recovered from the change from the lira. Let's leave that to the Italians! I have to hand it to the Italians. The food is amazing, the suits are suave, the cars are sleek, the ladies are gorgeous, and the men are steely. The most stylish in the world other than the Irish. The Italians have Ferraris. The Irish have racehorses, Guinness and oysters! We are legends in our own mind.

In 2007 land values had reached an incredible high in Ireland and were rising further. Being a conservative type, we purchased sites that were within our financial reach without overextending our capability in the early 2000s. Profitable sites. Two years before 2007 and developers were buying sites for

€10 million. Planning to build 200 homes. Their accountants were telling the banks that they needed another €50 million to buy another site near Dublin. The attitude was: shovel the money out to us, charge what you like on interest, take your super-inflated arrangement fee and bonus, roll up the interest for 12 months with an extension period. The collateral was the future stock not yet built on that €10 million site.

We, the conservatives, were looking for a few hundred thousand and we were watching the interest rate and the arrangement fee. We questioned it. We got lambasted and were asked what was wrong with us by bank managers! This is the rate and that's that was the mantra. We argued. We were not popular at all. We were, after all, businessmen and knew our game. It didn't seem like we knew anything when we were talking to the bank. They were the experts or so they thought! All was revealed later about how clueless these people were and how little they understood about basic economics. I still question it today. Borrowed time is not sustainable when it comes to finance and loan structures.

One time I saw an auction to build 13 houses on a site. It was 2006. The site was up for auction for €1.4 million. It sold for €2.1 million plus 9% stamp duty. Say €2.3 million for approximate sake. So, the total earnings on the project for 13 houses @ €300,000 = €3.9 million. The build cost was going to be €150,000 per unit which amounted to €1,950,000 plus €2,300,000 = €4,250,000. A loss of €350,000. The bust came and those houses were half-finished. The developer was well bust and probably ended up in NAMA. This was the National Asset Management

Agency, which was set up in Ireland to try to manage the assets and liabilities of the bank by the government. I suppose they were protecting the bailout package that they gave the banks. These wonderful banks that knew what they were doing… NOT!

The accidental emigrant!
Ireland
THE GREAT RECESSION

Corporate culture – uncultured people

This was the 2007 run. The shit hit the fan in America. Then like a common cold it spread. The global markets were in flux and we were to all intents and purposes sitting ducks and we did actually know what we were doing. All that bank bullshit about borrow more, front-loading loans etc that we were hearing a few years earlier. Absolute crap. We were told by one business manager that we were a pain in the arse because we only wanted to borrow a small amount of money and we also wanted the best rate. That equates to good business in my estimation: big profit, low borrowings. Not quite, according to the banking sector. We all know now what happened. I asked a business manager when I was in this meeting, "How are the bank going to fix the melt down problem?" The business manager told me to watch the TV and read the newspapers. Not only were they a crass bunch, but also quite thick. Rabbit in the headlights stuff. No gold stars for managing your affairs in a measured and businesslike manner. This kind of treatment enraged me. I'd say if you had the lowest IQ in the world you could be in the running for a top job in any bank in Ireland. By that I mean CEO. As the saying goes, visualise! All you need to do is shovel out money, be completely corrupt, let others brainwash you that you are right even when you are morally bankrupt, have no idea how to count, and try to hold onto your arse you can't find with both hands and you have the job.

The accidental emigrant! Ireland
THE GREAT RECESSION

The oversight by the financial sector!
Like a rabbit in the headlights the business manager couldn't equate how we differed from our friend the €50 million man and his brilliant accountant. The man was borrowing on the strength of green fields. We, on the other hand, were men, measured, hard-working and in most cases calculating our investments six to 12 months at a time to the turnaround. Money paid etc... We, a different-coloured lobster, were dropped into the boiling water with the careless lobsters and left to boil in the same pot.

In any other industry job credentials of a bank manager like the one I described wouldn't sustain a person for more than a week. Governments were broke. We were watching the construction industry in the space of six months disintegrate. We did some small projects. For a little while we made a living. A few relatives asked us to do some construction work. That was a godsend. Then the work dried up.

The fallout! I essentially had to pack my bag and head for London, England. I was lucky. I had a neighbour who helped me get an interview with a construction engineering firm in London. They gave me the job straight away. I was the man for the job. A dramatic change for me. Life in London is work to bed. Life is very quick! I would shower at night to save time in the morning. Up at 5am, dressed in under ten minutes and out of the door. It was a terrifying time, to be honest. Pressure of paying the bank sharks, drowning in a mountain of debt and living in another country away from your spouse. Real pressure if you are trying to honour your commitment. Other people emigrated in the past and it was hard for them, too. They probably worked on the lump and rarely ever saw their families again. They might have had a lonely existence but hadn't a mountain of debt. If they had a good head and were steady, the only way was up. I suppose I had a mountain of debt and the banks wanted to kill me! As Keith Flint said, "Feel the pressure, come play my game, I'll test ya." They did…

London
THE ACCIDENTAL EMIGRANT! THE GREAT
RECESSION

Life had become tough. England was in a recession, too! Things were bad here. Money was tight and there were cuts everywhere. Tower cranes were rusting in the skyline. Miles away from where I was in Ireland. A successful building contractor. A well-educated civil engineer that knew a lot about his industry. It would all have remained that way if a few idiots in charge of the financial industry were paid **not** to work.

But that's life. Idiots get on and don't pay the price for failure. They say the following about power in the wrong hands.

"Power in the hands of a fool is a dangerous tool." You could also say it this way – **"Power in the hands of a tool is a dangerous fool!"**

Yes, that's right: the dangerous fool was the financial wizard who invented sub-prime non-repayable mortgages! A busy fool not being watched is even more treacherous. The funny thing is now that non-repayable mortgage is for a set of wheels. Car sub-prime mortgages. Let's hope that the financial whizz kids have calculated this one right. When you work at the bottom you know everything about life. You have lived!

These apes got promoted for failure and a couple of million of a **bonus** and **no jail time!** I want a job like that! Talking shit about big arrangement fees, front-loading loans and complete bollocks about future green field business plans of complete hot air. The result of this poncing and prancing around, you ask?

Half-built housing estates and shopping centres built in places where people were leaving in search of a job before the bust. In Ireland in 2006 we were constructing 90,000 homes a year. In Britain they were building 95,000 homes a year. Britain had 60 million of a population in 2006, and Ireland had 4.5 million. You do the maths? Did anyone assess anything, governments included? Governments are bankrupt when it comes to cop on!

The recession for me meant that I commuted on a fortnightly basis for about five years and then, as I got very busy in England, monthly. That commute would start at 4am on a Monday. Heading for Shannon Airport for the 6am flight. Michael O'Leary of Ryanair, a clever man, was counting on us to fill his planes. He adjusted the price and convenience for us to travel cheaply to another country. We were on-site in England at 8am or thereabouts after travelling in the middle of the night. Didn't sleep much either on Sunday night getting ready for the Monday return. I was on an adrenaline high most of the time to function. But then again, I had bills and most of all mortgages to pay the bank. So, going to England on Monday at 4am and coming home on Friday at 9pm a month later was a must. Spend Saturday taking a few calls with problems to be sorted in England then cut the grass, have a few pints and it's Monday morning!

There was a long period when I was a project manager in charge of constructing high-rise blocks in Central London for an Irish subbie. On these projects that's where I went to bed for a few hours. Say four, for argument's sake. They were high-pressure projects. Highly charged! I applaud anyone who is a concrete frames contractor in London trying to grow a business. In Ireland there are approx. five million people in the whole country. In London there are double that population in a city. Think of the logistics of getting gear in and out of a site in Central London. Concrete, shuttering, steel, men, tools, fencing gates and an array of materials. Then there is the money and staying ahead of the game. Not easy at all.

London
THE ACCIDENTAL EMIGRANT. THE GREAT RECESSION

The Logistics game of London & Concrete!
In London there is Tom, Dick and Harry on a scooter, bike or on foot trying to nail you to the cross with parking tickets. Noise control and no place to park. The streets are tight and there is zero space to store materials. You would sometimes be taking a flyer and land a load of gear in an empty lot belonging to someone else for a few hours just because you were about to burst under pressure. Build a floor in a week or even two was the target. I had a notepad by my bed to write notes in the middle of the night when I woke up in a sweat, thinking, did I remember that etc…? 150 men on the job and no time. 16 weeks and six acres of floor space in a building. Information slow and the programme still on target. We have come and gone. Lost count of how many loads of concrete and how many articulated lorries came through the gates. On a big construction site you had at least 12 men at your office

at 7 in the morning with genuine problems. Steel drawings not tallying. Building dimensions not correct. Conflicting elements! The rest of the men waiting at my office at 7am would be there asking for petty stuff. Well, you would just tell them to get lost! Too much pressure and not enough time. We had this job warts and all. Tough job!

The engineer for the main contractor who was a busy little bastard would be breaking my balls over something absolutely irrelevant. The drawings had been outsourced about six times as there was a recession going on and the main outfit were busy trying to save money. Not only that, there were supposed to be three tower cranes on the job and they only installed one. Sometimes it took two days to get a response to a request for further information on a mistake on some drawing. The consulting engineer happened to be in **New Zealand**! Think of the time difference. On the site and more shuttering and pans required asap and some lad broke some tool yesterday and we need that tool right now as we are pouring concrete in 40 minutes. Oh yeah on that last one, let me look down my pants and see if I can just pull one out. On this particular day we had a $1000m^3$ concrete pour and the poker vibrator for vibrating the concrete packed up. That's a hundred grand's worth of concrete.

Unknown to me at the time, the other two spare pokers in our site store were broken. It was going to take too long for a hire company to get to us and the concrete would be too hard to vibrate by then. We needed to keep pumping the concrete as the pour was timed and organised. If there was a delay in the concrete pour it would screw up the travel times and sequence of the truck returns from the concrete batching plant. The concrete would as a direct result take longer. Hours longer. That meant more lights to work late into the night or even the next day. Concrete gangs will understand when shit happens! It usually is not their fault. It is some hapless fool that causes the problems or maybe a breakdown of sorts. Ask the Punjab boys. They know all about this stuff!

The Logistics game of London & Concrete.

A delay would also screw up the concrete pump as any downtime would allow the concrete to dry out in the concrete hosepipes, making it harder to pump when the concrete pumping would resume. I was sweating bullets. You couldn't make it up! I jumped in my jeep and raced towards other jobs with tower cranes visible on the skyline. I got to the nearest job. I met the foreman who was from Dublin.

That helped my situation. He knew all about what it was like to be in the shit... I had taken out any bank cards that had funds from my wallet. It had about £100 in cash in it and a few other bank cards with no funds which I left in it. I gave him my wallet and watch as security for the poker vibrator. He gave me the tool and off I raced back to the site. The job in question was a continuous concrete pour of a concrete post-tensioned floor so we had only so much time to vibrate the concrete or we would have what you call honeycombing on the floor soffit. 160 lorry loads of concrete is nothing to be sniffed at. For every day we go over the time on the job remember it's a £10,000 fine. The concrete was poured. We are sorted for another day!

To add to the colour on these jobs, the canteen smelled like an international food market. Salty Romanian sausages to Indian yellow dal. Polish pork to an English breakfast. What a culture. The great thing about men on construction sites is they talk to each other and there is very little bullshit tolerated.

Not long after that one Christmas I was going to work in Hertford at 5am. It was minus 20 outside. Not to mention that I nearly wrote the car off a few times on the way. I remember when we got to the job, it was so cold that I was feeling real pain. I along with the rest of the workforce was working hard to keep myself warm by jumping up and down. Three jumpers, two coats, long johns, heavy jeans, three pairs of socks and still cold. An inch of ice on the floors of the building. Forget work, let's get a pair of skates.

The financial collapse brought these great experiences to me. I am not complaining. **When someone throws lemons at you, add sugar and make lemonade, then piss in it and give it to the bank manager. Maybe slip him a few e tablets, too, and he could go on another trip**!

The first trip only got him promoted. He didn't get a bonus in 2008. A life less than ordinary had started and there is a lot more fun and games to come. Big stories from London! But first you have to experience the most interesting of Ireland's characters!

The remainder of this book is dedicated to all the

construction characters and people whom I came into contact with in more than one country. I hope you enjoy the rest of this book. We now meet Irish characters and Irish stories.

Chapter 6

Ireland

CHARACTERS 1!

Irish Characters I met along the way during the 1990s
A Story about Mick "The Pony", the son and me. Paints a
picture of the 1990s

It was the year of 1996. I had just left university and it was time
to get out to work. The real world... I got a job with a good
rival housebuilder. My first job was working on groundwork
with Mick Conlon. Mick was a low-sized man about 5' 6" in
height with a pot belly, big, Popeye arms and hands the size
of shovels. He was a leader! A gruff man by nature. He had
worked in England for about 30 years before I met him. He
was 55 years old and a tough nut. A type that will never be seen
again. He worked the bollocks off us. I remember the tips of
my fingers would be throbbing when I woke up in the morning
from the concrete burns. Small, little holes that appeared on
the tips of your fingers from concrete exposure.

Mick had a very gruff and aggressive side to him. If you
worked you were alright. If you didn't you were gone! He was
exceptional at his job and knew what he was doing. He trained

me well. Most new fellows got moved on, as they didn't make the grade in the first hour or two. He would head to the office at about 9 or 9.30am and then the foreman would appear in his van. The next thing you knew the new guy would be called away to sweep out houses or work elsewhere. Mick would guillotine them from the outset. Too small, too weak, too cheeky, no cop on, clueless. Just some of the words that Mick used to describe some of the new people who would be brought to him to work in our gang.

One particular day a cat had the misfortune of licking Mick's hand while he was cutting some floor insulation. Well, the cat was sorry he ever walked up along the wall of that pair of semi-detached houses. Mick hit the cat an almighty wallop when the cat licked his hand. Not only that, he also growled at the cat like a dog. Mick had two sons. Pat who was about 30 and a superb concrete man, and Mick junior who was a recently qualified quantity surveyor. He was more cultured than the other two. He was calm, clever and reserved. An absolute gent. I had the pleasure as a budding professional to be working alongside him.

The story of Mick Junior is that we were in the canteen one day having our lunch break. The canteen, by the way, was a 20'-long shipping container with blocks on the floor and a few scaffold boards as the seat laid on top of the blocks. Mick used to sit at a table inside the window and he used to nosily look out the window at the comings and goings outside and comment on what he saw. This one particular day his son started rummaging with a Dunnes Stores plastic bag. He was making considerable noise at a moment when the conversation between all the men went quiet. Mick (The Pony) piped up what have you in that bag that you are making such racket. What are you eating? The son Mick Junior, who was a chubby, heavy-set lad, responded, Chocolate bars, not that it is any of your business! The men's eyes were on stalks. You didn't say much to Mick Snr. Mick let a roar out of him. Put away them chocolate bars! You are as fat as fuck! He continued, it would be more in your line to be eating an orange or an apple. You are turning into a right auld fat knob of lard! he growled.

The guy sitting next to me (Specs) whispered to me, Who needs enemies when you have Mick as your father? The Pony kind of heard him. He challenged Specs: Don't be fucken whispering! If you want to say something, well, then say it. Specs continued to laugh. Specs turned to me and said, You are up. Specs didn't like Mick. They were hard workers but polar opposites. Specs was always riling me as a joke to ask Mick about all the men he put down in Camden Town in his young fighting days. Mick, I enquired, while trying to hold back the fit of laughing both I and Specs had, Tell us about all the lads in Camden Town that you busted up. What the fuck would you know about Camden Town? he retorted. When I was in Camden Town you were playing with your shit on the kitchen floor. Cheeky, little spoiled bastard! The whole container started laughing. He even laughed himself. The fit of laughing stopped for me.

I was aware now that when I went back to work Mick was going to break my balls for the next two weeks at least for being a sarcastic pup. Mick sacked the millionaire company owner's son and described him as a useless good-for-nothing ape to his father. Brave man. He also had many enemies on the site that he wouldn't work with. He wouldn't care if he was sacked. He was too productive to be sacked.

The day would start at 8am and a new fellow would appear for work. He would ask, Who is Mick? I am here to start work with Mick. Mick would look at the fellow. He would be sizing him up to see if he was strong enough or whether he had the cut of a worker or a bit of savvy. First he would be asking where he worked before. What he was doing. And then he would tell him to stay or go. If he stayed, then he would give the newbie a job to do. Then it would be, "How long more are you going to take at that job?" Then about 9.30am he would come around and Mick would disappear up the site and then the foreman would appear and take that lad away. There was a time when about three lads a week were being moved on. We were under pressure to do the foundations and floors of ten houses a week over a 20-house stretch, on our own in a six-day week. If the excavator was busy I would lift the 16-stone plate compactor over the wall myself. That's 200 weight. Heavy for a lad that weighs 9 stone. A gang of only three men we were! We turned out a lot of work on that job. In less than six months we were up at about 90 houses and that's considering that the site had to be stripped from a green field first.

I used to arrive at that site at 6.30 in the morning on cold, wet winter mornings and then mix about ten gauges of mortar before 7.30am with a guy we nicknamed the Guiding Star, or Guiden' for short. The reason we called him that was he had one cross eye so we didn't know where to look when we were trying to talk to him. Then at 7.30am I would open 80 houses for the tradesmen. Then we would get to work with Mick! A real bundle of laughs. NOT!

Ireland 1997
RICHIE THE CRANE DRIVER AND THE NEAR-CATASTROPHIC COLLISION SHOCK!

I secured a job as an engineer the following year and I got a job on a city high-rise project. My friend Richie the tower crane driver received an unmerciful shock one day on this job. The tower crane in the site next door was lifting a very large shuttering pan that the carpenters had completed. The day was windy and we were probably operating outside the wind limits. The guy next door started to lift this big shutter off the deck. The minute he lifted it off the deck it started into a big swing. The crane driver quickly continued to lift up the shutter pan. It quickly started to wave erratically, endangering the safety of the men on the deck. So, he lifted the shuttering pan even quicker and slewed to his left. At this point the shuttering pan was thrust into a full-scale, violent spin and was pulling the jib of the crane towards our building.

I was on the top floor of our building. First there was a huge bang. The building I was in shook. Then I observed the banksman in front of me. The steel mortar bin he was chaining up to our crane was hurriedly shunted off at speed and out through a fully finished, three-metre-high masonry wall. The wall was gone! Then there was a second bang and a sound of chains tangling. The wall had landed on a concrete flat roof four floors below us. By the Grace of God there was no one on that flat roof. It had been raining heavily and all the men were taking shelter out of the rain. Then the banksman said that his thumb was bleeding. I rushed to help him. The top of his finger had been torn badly by the chain.

I commanded another work colleague to get him to the ground floor to the foreman. Treat him and get him to hospital. I took the radio. The chains of our crane and the jib of the next-door crane were all mashed up. There was a mortar bin in a tangle in mid-air. It was a mess. The shuttering pan of the crane next door was hanging precariously over the top of a gable wall of our building. It didn't look good EITHER!

I radioed my friend Richie, the crane operator. Come in, Richie. No response. Hey, Richie. Are you OK? No response! Eventually. Pat, I am weak! I went back and over almost two metres when he hit me. I pinged like an elastic band. I thought I was a "gonner", he sighed. Totally shocked! Can't speak! Aw he was sighing! By the Grace of God that crane didn't fall over. Luck! That happened at about 2.30pm in the day. The two crane drivers eventually cut loose the tangle from each other. The men on-site nicknamed the crane driver next door Barbie because he was about 4' 6" in height. He was so small the men on his jobsite said he resembled a doll. They maintained that he was so small he needed cushions under his arse to see out the window, even though the window is below you. That wasn't his first offence. He had already pulled up a skip from the street a few weeks earlier and pulled it up through power lines and set a number of cars and a street on fire. Now Cyril the banksman was involved in that incident, too! I will tell all about Cyril later. The daft git! It was 4.30pm and all the men were heading home. No crane to lift materials.

Ireland

Richie the crane driver appeared at the door of the office. Are you alright, Richie? I enquired. I will when I get this baby up and running again. This guy was dedicated. He continued that he had called the crane company that erected the crane directly after the incident. They told him it would be at least three weeks before they would be able to come to fix it. He said we can fix it ourselves. I said, No, let's leave it to the experts. As senior engineer I have spoken to the board (me) and they have made an executive decision and it's a No. He said, I have erected loads of these cranes and I have the necessary papers to service them. Even still No! He persisted and then he was telling me that I was going to assist him. I laughed at the concept. Not a f***ing hope. He said, what are we going to do for the next three weeks here with no tower crane? We have no space for a mobile crane etc…

Fast-forward 20 minutes and Richie and I are going up the ladder of the crane. Now you have two dedicated idiots. When I passed out the top of the building and was completely exposed to the elements, I froze on the ladder with fright. First of all, it was blowing a gale-force wind. Second of all I never felt as exposed with little or no protection. I had a harness on but I was a bit exposed. We got to the cab and he showed me all the naked centrefolds on the wall of the cab before we headed out along the jib. A little playboy room in the sky. He was walking casually along the jib about 200ft off the ground. I, on the other hand, was crawling on the inside of the triangle of the jib. I was as nervous as hell.

Anyway, to cut to the chase we took out the pin that secured one of the flywheels to the trolley block, pulled the rope back over the flywheel and reattached it. All this time, the crane was blowing in different directions on free slew. When you are not operating the crane you must leave it on free slew. This is to allow the jib to move freely with the wind. This is to prevent the crane blowing over in stormy conditions. I was delighted, to be honest. It was 8pm and I wanted to hit home. I said, That's great, I am off. Not yet, he replied.

He said, Now we have to fix the hook block below which still has the mortar bin hanging from it. Richie dropped the skip back down on the top floor of the building. I detached the ropes from the skip. He then trolleyed out the ropes and put on the brakes for a few minutes. We then got into a one-cubic-metre concrete skip next door and Barbie the crane driver next door lifted us up about 100ft in the air where we pulled the hook block into the skip and proceeded to pull the wire rope back over the flywheel there, too. Then Richie got back in the crane and dropped the chains onto a quiet road and we examined the damage to the ropes. There were two strands sheared in 100, which equates to 1 in 50. The crane company allowed us to operate on a temporary basis, doing a daily check on them to ensure that the ropes didn't deteriorate any further. Three weeks later the ropes were replaced. The moral of this story was that we were rewarded for our efforts. I didn't expect anything. We both received an extra pay cheque that week for our efforts. The company would stand to lose £75,000 per week if there was no production on-site. I genuinely don't know how I even had the balls to agree to do what I did. In today's world we would never have been allowed to do such. Accident and incident reports as well as the HSE would be priority. Different times!

The stand-in banksman, concrete and cars

We had problems retaining banksmen on the job at that time. The dot-com boom was in full swing and there was a shortage. One day my friend Richie asked me to bank the crane for an hour or two as the banksman walked out. I agreed. There was a concrete pour going on. I got in the basket of a ride on concrete skip. This is a skip that you stand in a man basket and travel with the skip. There is a wheel in front of you and you turn it slightly to open the door and let the concrete escape. It would flow into a rubber tube and into a column box. When the pour finishes and you are ready to go to the street for the next load; the tube would be tied back on itself to stop any concrete dropping off onto cars, pedestrians or workmen. The concrete gang on the floor failed to tie it up and I couldn't see the tube.

As we slewed over this open private car park I could hear a tick-ticking sound. It happened about three times. I eventually looked over the skip and onto the ground. I could see the cars in this car park were absolutely peppered with concrete spots. Panic! I knew that the car park owner was a complete wanker and there would be lawsuits coming out our arse if I didn't wash the cars quick. As soon as we hit the ground I was out of the cage. I pulled a hose across the street as far as I could. I rounded up three men and a few buckets. We were running at the cars and just drowning them in water only. No cloths. We did it. A hot dry day and all the cars are wet! The owner arrived back to the car park. He was scratching his head. We stopped the pour until he left and we drew him to figure out what was going on. The guy I would say genuinely wondered: did it just shower over his car park? Lucky!

I would like to say that I salute those people who go 300 metres to one kilometre in the air and enter a cab in what can only be described as one of the most responsible jobs in construction. The crane driver. The crane supervisor and the banksmen are equally as important. A seriously responsible job. Respect.

Ireland 1996
CHARACTERS

Marty the painter and the wife's clothes
It was Christmas of 1996. We broke for the Christmas holidays on the 23rd of December. The gang of painters made up a number of seven or eight lads that worked for a subbie. They were all very brazen. Loads of cheeky chat out of them. These were real City slicker boys.

There were 100 men plus on this job and it was a busy site. There was this guy called Marty. Marty had a kind of squeaky, twanging voice and a real handlebar moustache. He was a sound fellow but a bit strange-looking if I am honest. The handlebars definitely added to the strange look.

The men he worked with decided to tell a story that unfolded during the holidays. Marty had a daughter and a son. The daughter was in school before Christmas and the teacher asked all the kids in the class to draw a lovely family picture for Christmas.

Marty's daughter drew her picture of the "family". The teacher asked her to tell her who were the people in the picture. She started by saying, Well, this is my brother Johnny, he is four. This is me. This is my mammy and this is my daddy. The teacher responds, This is fine but Mommy wears a guna (dress) and Daddy wears briste (trousers). But Daddy is wearing a dress? Why is this? The child responds... When Mommy goes to Tesco on a Thursday night, Daddy goes to her wardrobe and tries on her dresses.

The first day back after the holidays the painters ran around the job and told everyone what had happened during the Christmas break. One of the other painters' kids brought the story home from school. Then all the painters had the story. Like blooded hounds they were!

This was at a time when things were not like they are today. It was not as PC as it is today. Not a very pleasant place to be if you were outed as a cross-dresser in Ireland. Never mind Limerick City.

The men on the job were taunting him with: 5 dolla', 5 dolla', I love you long time. Kiss, kiss, Marty Sparkey. How is your Gee, Marty? A reference to a woman's private parts.

They guy was a broken man. His mistake was **not** to deny it. In an environment like that he should have denied all knowledge of such an incident.

I was having my lunch in the front room of this house on a freezing cold afternoon when Marty walked in and broke down in tears. He said he was going to pack in his job and he couldn't take any more. I asked him had he another job. He said no but none of the men would work with him. I said that's a bonus. I wouldn't work with any of those wankers anyway.

I advised him to brave it out and work on. They will not pay your mortgage or the schoolbooks for your children. Fuck them. He did but I would say it was tough. In the mid-1990s in Ireland people were not as open as today!

Chapter 7

Ireland 1993
THE POTEEN-MAKERS. PHÁIRT.

This is the story of my introduction to "The Poteen Makers"!
At the age of 19 I was into my fifth year on sites during the summer holidays. I was working on a building site in Limerick in Ireland. On my first day of the holidays I arrived for work at 7.45am. I called at the site office where I was greeted by the company secretary. I told her that I was reporting for my first day of work. I was informed that I was to wait outside the site office for the foreman. I waited and waited. At 8.45am the foreman burst out of his office. A two-metre-tall, two metres in diameter, red-faced and bad-tempered man with a thick Derry accent no less. Are yeou Pat? he asked in his Northern accent. Yes, I responded. Get in the von. That's van. A Red Toyota Hiace van. I diligently obeyed his forceful request.

He drove down through this big building site asking a few basic pleasantries. They weren't questions as such, more like, this is my site and you abide my rules, was what his body language suggested. I had met his kind before! A complete dictator with a penchant for control. His way of progress was a dogmatic one which I would soon learn. We arrived at this almost complete house. His final words before we got out of the van were, Keep your head down and your arse up and you will be alright. I got it: work hard!

We arrived in the living room of this house and the dictator introduced me to these two country boys from County Clare who were having their tea break. Brian and Mick, father and son. "The Poteen Makers". The foreman used to call them the flying squad as he maintained that they were so high from the poteen that they could fly.

The foreman would instruct scaffolders to start taking down scaffolding early, before the roof was complete just to piss off the poteen boys. The foreman was giving me once again my pep talk that no prisoners would be taken here. The two poteen makers were sort of sniggering albeit very faintly and both looked like they had a permanent grin on their faces. I knew what they were at but played the obedient servant. He eventually left the house and the two lads started talking. They asked me about myself and then swiftly moved onto the foreman. What was the Englishman on about? He is only down here because they don't want him up the north, they commented. Who does he think he is anyway?!

They were having a sandwich and Mick the father said, You will have a drop of poteen. I, being innocent, laughed. Mick got thick with temper. What are you laughing at he asked me. I said, You know poteen and all that! He vexedly said to his son, Brian, go and get the bottle from the car and I will show this eejit that we are "no lightweights". Cheeky pup! You must remember that pure poteen was a banned substance in Ireland. It was illegal to make it. It's 100% proof.

The son brought back a Hennessy brandy bottle wrapped in brown paper. It contained within it a clear, water-like liquid. I laughed and said very funny lads, that's water. Again, Mick got thick. He put the bottle up to my nose. It smelled like treacle mixed with very potent whiskey. The joke was over. He poured a drop into his cup of tea, the son's cup of tea, and then mine. At that very moment the father said, Quick, hide the bottle, Paisley (foreman) is coming back.

By Paisley they meant the Northern Irish red-faced, bad-tempered, jowl-shaking foreman George. To briefly explain. The Reverend Ian Paisley was an elected British Unionist politician in Northern Ireland famous for his line, "Ulster Says No". He was also a bit of a dictator! This foreman George was his twin.

The son Brian was running around the front room of this house like a headless chicken. Panicking like hell! He eventually hid the bottle in under the stairs in the hall. Paisley burst through the front door at a rate of knots and roared, Youz boyz are drinkin' again! The father rose to his feet like a terrier denying all knowledge and breaking into a tirade of abuse. Mick was a man who was as thin as a lath and of a wiry nature. The big fella (Paisley) and the chief poteen maker were abusing each other with passion. Two alphas going at it without fists. The difference between these two characters was that the poteen maker was a kind sort with a great sense of humour and comedy. The other lad was dark in humour and driven by success and status. A very stressed-out character! The foreman left the house shouting if I catch youz boyz drinkin on the job you will going down the road. In other words you will be sacked. He had no intention of it. They were very good at their job.

When he eventually left the house the son burst out laughing. The father, who was still high from temper and like a man possessed, said, We will drink today, tomorrow, next week, next month and next year and that Englishman won't catch us. Now you must remember that I was only in these fellows' company for about 20 minutes. I didn't know what to think. It was something of a baptism of fire.

We finished up our tea. Later, I was on the roof loading the roof tiles while standing on the roof battens and my chest started pounding. I was a fit guy. I never drank a drop of alcohol. I said to Mick that my heart was racing and thumping. I think I am having a heart attack. He laughed with passion and said, We'll make you a man yet. He suggested that when the roof was loaded to get some water. This actually quelled the heart palpitations for a while but it resumed later. He maintained that he drank a tumbler of it daily and that when they dig him up in hundreds of years he will still look the same as he is now. A funny man! This was only the beginning of my time with these lads. I had a whole summer to put down with them. It was very entertaining. A comedy sketch on a daily basis.

Ireland

THE POTEEN BOYS AND THE GERMAN. ZWEITER TEIL.

This story is one of humour and, well, things that get lost in translation. We were roofing this house on a luxury housing estate. That's me, the head poteen maker Mick and his son Brian. The Derry foreman came to the house where we were working on Friday afternoon and called the head poteen maker down from the roof. I could see after a minute the conversation wasn't going well and there was a lot of head-shaking and finger-pointing. I thought it was going to get interesting. I commandeered the son to get closer within earshot of the conversation. We hid on the scaffold quietly and listened. It went like this.

Mick. HPM. (Head poteen maker and father of the duo): I am not doing it.

Foreman: Monday at 8am, you just be there. I am not arguing with you. You have your orders.

Mick – HPM: I am not going up on that roof. I didn't roof that house. Durkin the bullock with his size 13 boots, gallon belly and fat head roofed that house. Fat bastard. He wouldn't roof a fucking hen house. That's what happens when you get a bull of a plasterer, remove him from his environment and put him above all places but on a roof. It's all your fault that the fat man pierced the felt with his moccasins, he growled. You couldn't wait for us professionals and in our place you thought an amateur could do it. You bloody fool!

This Construction Life

Foreman: Monday at 8. The end!

Mick: NOT A HOPE!

They both departed from each other. Cranky as a bag of cats. Mick just wittering away under his breath as usual. Expletive after expletive.

Monday morning. The scene!

Monday morning comes and we are diligently waiting in a red Citroën CX car outside the house of this German fellow. A right old banger of a car too. The red "VON" pulled up and the gruff Derry man gets out. He had brought with him a roll of felt, a gallon of bitumen and some brushes. We knew that this was going to be a complete bitch of a job. What we had to do was go up into the attic, cut the roll of felt into strips, then roll on some liquid bitumen and then slip it down between the rafters. A shitty, dirty job.

We approached the front door of the house. The door opened and the woman of the house who was a portly, stern-looking lady with a red face peered out through a slightly ajar door. She straight away started a rant at the foreman. She wasn't happy with this and that. He basically in a gruff manner told her like it or lump it. In his Derry accent he growled that it was the only house in the estate where there was a track in the ground from his site office to her front door. He had enough and walked away. The head poteen maker had this permanent smile on his face while all this was going on. He loved the aggravation that the foreman was receiving. Which, I might add, was a sight in itself. Mick had about three teeth missing on top and bottom of his mouth. He smoked a tobacco rollies called Sweet Afton. This and the poteen were contributing factors. The man relished the fact that the foreman was getting a lambasting. No love lost there!

We made a move to enter the house. The tradesmen's entrance is around the back, the plump lady snapped with her red face and jowls shaking with temper. Just as we were making our way through the back door Mick quipped to the lady that he was here to do a job under duress and that he would not have another episode like the one at the front door. The lady retorted irately, what did he mean? He just asked had she taken her tablets when she rose out of bed. He then proceeded forward. Where is the access stairs to the attic? he enquired. This is the point the husband, a German fellow called Gunther, turned up. He was a thin man with wispy hair. He pulled down the attic stairs. When we eventually got into the attic the existing roofing felt had thousands of X's marked on it. Mick said, where are the O's? to the German. The German fellow didn't understand what Mick was saying.

He proceeded to tell us enthusiastically that it took him a day with the magnifying glass to ensure he marked all z holes with an X. Martin responded, Zat vwas a Vaste of time. Mick the joker proceeded to tell this German fellow that if he saw a problem he would fix it. It went like this: If ve see problem ve vill fix it. The German responded, Yes, I know. The German fellow continued why are you talking to me like this? I do understand English! Mick responded, Like Fwhat? The son was shaking his head. Oh here we go again, he smiled. Both myself and the son turned into a corner behind the chimney stack and held our noses as our faces nearly blew up trying to hold in our laughter.

We started to break into laughter at which point Mick dipped the brush in the gallon can of bitumen and said to the German, You arr holding vme uph. The German fellow proceeded to go down the ladder, saying, I don't know why you are talking to me like this. Martin under his breath made a remark about who won the war anyway?

When he was gone, Mick gave out yards to us. He said you are an awful bunch of fools. I had that lad going there. He was nearly gone mad. I had him so confused and then you idiots had to start into a big feckin skit. He irately continued, Jaysus, will I ever train yee idiots? Will you ever learn?

Five minutes later the wife arrived, shouting the odds about who was taking the mickey out of my husband. Mick crossly said, what are you on about? We are only doing our work here. To distract her thoughts away from the topic, he politely asked if she would make him a cup of tea, that his throat was a bit dry, only to get a response of certainly not from the bitch.

He said, she started this whole charade when she answered the door this morning and spoke to me the way she did. It's not over yet. There is a long day in it. Mick was the kind of fellow that would do his job excellently but he had a different way of suffering fools. They would have to catch up with him. It was harmless satire.

He was one of the most gifted and intelligent people I ever met. The German came up to the attic at the end of the day. He was trying to get more out of us. We had resolved all the issues and more. The German wanted more. Mick just said I will leave it to you. Good man! Any more problems and "Durkin Donut" is your man. I never in my life laughed as hard. We were driving down the road that evening and then it all came out. Mick himself burst out laughing. He laughingly said, Paisley will never be allowed to send us in there again! HA!

THE POTEEN MAKERS, THE OLD MECHANIC AND HIS STICKY TONGUE! PARTIE TROIS

The final story goes like this. These poteen boys were doing all the roofs on a big city apartment and house project in town. I was their labourer or summer apprentice, whatever way you looked at it. They had a problem with one of the petrol saws. We used this tool to cut the concrete roof tiles. They used to nickname it "the motorbike". Stuff like, pass me the motorbike, or Will you cut that batch of barge tiles with the motorbike? The motorbike broke! And in true joking style the father decided to go and ask this old fella that used to occupy a front room of an old tenement house in a backstreet nearby to fix it. This old boy was dressed like a blacksmith with the old worn French-style hat, a boiler suit and a cravat tie around his neck. Let's nickname him Frenchie, says Mick. The old boy used to repair old motors, motorbikes and anything electrical. I'd say he knew what he was doing!

Mick brought us for the fun of it. He started by asking the old fellow, You fix old motorbikes, do ya? The man sarcastically replied, Ah yeah, gesturing to all the motorbikes in the shop! Mick, "head poteen maker": What about one-wheeled motorbikes? The old boy looked amused. What are ya talking about? Then my man produced the concrete-cutting petrol saw. It had one wheel on it! He laughed. Then Mick said, now we have no money, but we are into bartering. I think Mick had a sixth sense and could pick out a piss pot from the crowd. Your man asked, what will you barter, then? Say three bottles of the finest poteen that ever graced the planet! The boy said, "Really?" Mick responded, we are the last of a dying breed. We are the very last authentic poteen makers in Ireland. They took their hobby seriously! Honestly, they were very good at their hobby and it "was totally illegal". They used to produce 90 bottles at a time. They made the stuff with passion. They were raided a few times but the Gardaí never looked in the spare oil tank in the garden! Clever boys.

Anyway, it was agreed. The price was set at three bottles of the hard stuff. It's great **tack**, the father said with a jovial smile. But go easy on it. That three bottles should do you a few months. Friday evening arrived and the motorbike was fixed and the mechanic got his bottles of tack. The following Monday there was no sign of the mechanic arriving for work. He drove an old Austin Cambridge that billowed out blue, stinky smoke. Tuesday no sign, Wednesday no sign. All the time the son was saying to the father, you killed the old codger, and a big laugh. Thursday and the old boy surfaced. I, being that naïve type, felt responsible for the old guy, even though I only observed the deal! The father shouted to the old boy, Did you enjoy the tack? I did, said the old boy. My tongue is still stuck to the top of my mouth. He enquired, Have ya any more of that, lads? The old boy had drunk at least three months' worth of stuff over the weekend. The Poteen boys were impressed. I was amused! Not only did I think he might have snuffed it, but also these two were ready to start peddling or bootlegging more absolutely illegal alcohol again....

Chapter 8

Irish Characters
IRELAND 1997

John 3:7 and the rifle incident.

We were working on that same site as the Richie and crane incident. I was friendly with a fellow called John. He was an electrician. He was nicknamed John 3:7, something about his clairvoyant powers! He was a great guy. He loved going shooting in his spare time. Shooting pheasants or deer at the weekend. This one day he arrived in work and unknown to me brought the gun.

At lunchtime I went to the coffee shop for my lunch. At 1.30pm when I arrived back the door of the office was shut. The foreman and I never closed the site office door. Upon opening the door, I saw a timber gun case on my desk and immediately thought, what is this box? Then there was John with the gun cocked behind the door. He was angry, or so I thought. He roared at me that I was a prick and I was to get down on the floor. I sort of joked with him. Jaysus John, come on, what is this about? He lunged forward, pushing the gun to my head and told me to get on my knees on the ground and hold my hands up over my head. I dutifully did as he requested. All the time I was thinking, this guy is gone nuts. I was worried. Very worried! I knew this guy only a few months so I wasn't sure about the situation. In my worried state I got angry and said, Well, if you are going to fucking shoot, then shoot, you bollocks. He was frothing at the mouth. Then he started laughing and about ten other lads on the job that were in on the joke all burst into the office and roared, Ha, we got you, you moron! They were laughing at me, taunting me about my statement, Go on then shoot, you bollocks. Lads on sites can be cruel bastards!

I found it not at all amusing. I nearly got sick with the fright of it. I never had a gun pointed at me before and I froze. It was a squeaky bum moment. All the blood drained out of my face. I looked like a ghost I was so pale from the shock. A memory I would like to erase.

John 3:7 The pub, the redhead, and John's "Johnson"
John was the one at the butt of this story. We were coming close to finishing that project and we decided to go for a few pints on a Friday night in a busy nearby pub. Myself, John and another few lads were having pints. These four girls walked in and John in his true devilment challenged me. I dare you to go over there and try and chat them birds up. You have to pull one of them. He then said, you haven't a fucking hope! Ordinarily I may not have had a hope. I took him up on his dare. This time I had a plan! I said, No bother. I will charm those birds off the trees. I was no smooth-talker. As I walked away from them,

I could see the bollix and the other two laughing their nuts off, thinking that I would fail. Fuck them, I thought. I coolly walked over and started off with, Hi, ladies, my name is George Best, how are you all tonight? They laughed. I asked them to be cool, smile and wave to those three wankers over in the corner. There are four drinks of your choice in it for you if you go with it. They went with it. I called the barman and told him to fill whatever drink they wanted. I said, If you can tolerate me for a few minutes more it would be very much appreciated. One of the girls, a real stunner, said, I can do one better than that, love. She leaned over and planted a smacker on my cheek. I called them over at that point: I had pulled.

John and one of the girls, a redhead with beautiful green eyes, hit it off almost immediately. I thought no more of it. We were 23 and this lady was at least 32. The next Monday arrived and he said he had a rough weekend and that his Johnson was hanging off. She nearly broke the fella. Another week or two passed. He says he is loving this lady. He is having the best sex of his life and she just can't keep her hands off him. Not a bad problem to have, I thought. I didn't expect the next part of this story.

The only thing was she didn't tell him that she was married with two kids. Screech! That's me pulling the needle across the record. The party is over. We are onto the third week and this chunky, heavy-set fellow arrives at the site looking for John Murphy. He was shouting stuff like he was going to kill him and stuff like he was having it off with my wife. I felt for this guy. I really did. I didn't like the fact that this girl hurt him. But John was my work colleague and I didn't want him to get a beating.

OK, maybe just a small one for pointing the gun at me!

I did, however, think that this chunky fellow thought John Murphy was on this site. If he got him, he would beat him senseless. Probably kill him. I told him out of all the fellows that are here we don't have anyone by the name of John Murphy. He eventually went away. After an hour or so! My man was on the first floor looking out and probably left the entire contents of his bowels in his underpants. He was absolutely shitting bricks. He said by that week he had his suspicions about her. At which point she went a bit cool on him. Close call. After he held me up at gunpoint, I should have shown the fella in to get some retribution. I just averted two lads getting more hurt! Lucky man, John! You could say he was firing his guns and one of them backfired on him.

Ireland

Paudie O', the drugs and the Derry foreman.
I met this fellow called Paudie on-site in 1997. He was a labourer. A very hard worker and an even harder drug taker. He was one of these fellows that lived for the weekend. He was a really wild, motivated fellow. Mad as a brush and loved his drugs. He was a man who loved his E's and speed. I'd say the speed never wore off. Not only did he speak at 100mph, but he also worked as fast. It was a wet, overcast Monday morning at work. Lashing rain. I had missed work the previous week as I had the flu. I was bordering on pneumonia. On that very Monday, I was instructed by the Derry man to go down into a

block of terrace houses with my partner in crime young Mick, the Pony's son, and deck out the first floor with plywood and prop the joists of a block of terrace houses.

The concrete blocks were being delivered in 30 minutes. We worked like dogs for 40 minutes. Two young, fit fuckers! We collectively had the first house decked out with plywood and all the central span of joists propped. This was to allow the joists to take the weight of the concrete blocks that were being delivered. The bricklayers were a rough bunch and their chief was an ignorant sort. He hadn't any culture in him. We noticed on the first house that the stairwell was missing. I quickly went to the grumpy foreman and notified him that there was no stairwell (an opening on the first floor in which you would locate your stairs) in any of the three terrace houses. He had got two Northern Irish fellows to install the joisting over the weekend. However, they forgot to put in the opening for the stairs. A mistake that he would pay for in jokes by the site population.

It was Monday morning and he was as grumpy as fuck. He told me in no uncertain terms to get out and resume my work. I did. The chief bricklayer was causing uproar when I returned. He complained that he wasn't making any money and that we were holding him up and that there were no stairwells etc… The point is Paudie was tending five masons on his own and he was doing a great job of it. They were all busy working. He had inherited a Walter Mitty character the previous Friday and he was trying to train up this less than green fellow. A clumsy lad with no common sense at all! No place for such a fellow.

The foreman arrived down to where we were working on this big site and started ripping into Paudie. Paudie took the abuse. The bricklayer was shouting at the foreman now. The foreman was returning the abuse. It was all very uncivilised. Then the new apprentice was seen driving past some scaffold that Paudie had asked him to pick up earlier. He shouted over to Paudie, where is the scaffold located? He had just passed it out on the dumper twice. The next thing the foreman erupted into a complete tirade shouting, where do you think you are? On the number 7 bus? Then he made a beeline for this poor, unfortunate and called him a useless cunt and then fired him. The kid was so innocent he said, Will I go now? The foreman said, go to the gate, walk through it and never come back again. Will I come on Thursday to collect my last week's wages? You can guess the answer.

There were about 40 or so men witnessing this debacle in that particular corner of the site. The guy just put his head down, whimpered a bit and walked towards the canteen to collect his belongings. The guy was a Walter Mitty character but it was no way to talk to someone. It wasn't right! Some men were saying to the foreman, Disgraceful. You are an absolute pig another fellow roared.

What happened next, I didn't expect. He started into Paudie, at which point this normally jovial 100mph weekend drug taker decided to let rip. He took off his wellies (at great speed) that were laden with wet, slurry muck and threw them at the foreman and hit him in the chest of his suit jacket, while saying in slow motion: You can stick your job up your f***ing hole. He then proceeded to walk out through this filthy, mucky site in his socks like a cat on a hot tin roof.

Now the foreman had problems. No labourer to tend the five uncivilised bricklayers and no stairwell. Most of the problems were self-inflicted by the way he operated. The site all cheered and there was a huge eruption of laughter. This was the ultimate humiliation for the pig of the foreman. Then he started to aim for me, whom he disliked anyway. I just pointed to a saw that I had in my hand and said, Just don't. I continued: I can cut more than timber with the saw. He left. Unknown to me, I was duped into a house the next day by him. He threatened me that I was gone if I ever spoke to him like that ever again. Well, I told him that I was going back to work and that I would pretend that I didn't hear what he said. I just walked out. I never heard another thing about it. About a year later Paudie came into another job I was working on. He was looking for a job. I gave him a job. The guy could move mountains.

Chapter 9

Ireland 2000
IRISH CHARACTERS 4

Blondie Murphy and the collapse of the Odeon cinema in the capital.

The name has been changed to protect the identity of the individual in question. It is only fair to say that we might not be exactly accurate but you will get the drift! Blondie was nicknamed Blondie as he was looked a little like Clint Eastwood in the film *The Good, the Bad and the Ugly*. He was as cool as a breeze and he also used to rub the beard on his neck like Clint in the film. He was a real character. He was everything from a silage contractor to a builder. He was anything that turned a buck. He was a clever lad and he had men and machinery. Maybe too clever for his own good. His right hand didn't know what his left hand was doing! He would be a fellow to call if you wanted something underhand done. There was a developer that needed the Odeon cinema demolished. The council went against him on demolishing it, as it was a historic building. There was very little historic about this building. It was an eyesore.

Blondie either got the job or awarded himself to do a job in order to get the demolition contract. One Sunday morning at 6am, a tractor and trailer loaded with a 20-ton machine pulled up at the traffic lights for, say, five minutes. Apparently, some joyrider had accidentally got into the 20-ton digger that was still on the trailer and being towed by a tractor. It had been "apparently" stolen. That someone belted the shite out of the side of the building causing a partial collapse of the building onto the road. That someone had apparently stolen the tractor and trailer and then left the scene and parked it precariously at the back of a well-known local factory where all stolen cars would be found burned out. I am sure Blondie was after making a distressed call to the police notifying them of the theft of his machinery and the panic and upset of it all. No problem with the machinery. When the authorities found them they were fine. There were no keys in them, although the doors of the machines were open.

The local authority immediately gave a demolition notice and guess who got the contract? Blondie! Something tells me there was a lot more to it. There was a rancid smell about the whole debacle. The local authority gave a demolition notice at breakneck speed. This was the same authority that was restricting the demolition due to the buildings' so-called conservation status. Only God knows the truth on that one!

Ireland 1998

THE THIEVES AND THE FELLOW WITH THE STEERING PROBLEM

One day on this City high-rise project a few undesirables decided to break into our tool stores in broad daylight while the men were out on site. A passer-by saw them and alerted me that he saw two guys scaling the fence and then reappearing with petrol saws and heavy breakers. By the time I got to the stores they had scarpered. When the guy was alerting me, this wiry, aggressive fellow appeared out of the shadows and in a right cheeky accent started shouting at this old man. He was in his face, saying, Have you a 'steering problem'? Shouldn't you be going in another direction pops? Are you lost? I challenged this cheeky fellow, asking him to hang on while I called the lads down from the upper floors and you can tell them all about steering problems. The old fellow was well shook up by this degenerate. The lookout/degenerate wasn't long getting lost when I called the men down off the scaffold.

The bastards got pretty much every heavy-duty tool we had. We immediately called our security firm. The security guy arrived at 5.30pm and opened the boot of the car. He had all our tools. We were speechless. I was curious. I had to ask that burning question. How did you manage in the space of two hours to get all the equipment back? He responded, in our game you always must know a guy bigger than them. It's a game of who can intimidate who! I asked, did they give resistance? Let's say they will not be bothering you again. Nothing short of hospital treatment for those little runts, was his response. They won't be bothering you again, Paddy! Well, I thought, it was them who decided to break into our job. After all, they really frightened that old man. What's good for the goose is good for the gander.

On that same job that security guy saved one fellow from killing himself by deciding to climb up the crane in the middle of the night. He saved another from electrocuting himself while he tried to cut and rob a 3-phase electric cable that powered the tower crane. City jobs can bring all sorts of difficulties and complications. The underworld lurks in every city. Most people don't see it.

Ireland 2000
BOBBY G AND THREE TIMES A JOB!

Bobby G was a guy to whom I gave a labouring job. I gave him the job on the reference of a concrete truck driver who used to visit our site with concrete. By the state of his truck I shouldn't have warranted the reference.

Bobby G arrived to his first day of work. He arrived on an off-road trial bike with no helmet, no tax or insurance on the bike, and the silencer on the exhaust was broken. We could hear him coming for about a mile.

I put him to work immediately. He worked for the first two hours of the day diligently and I thought, OK, he might be alright. Break time came and he decided to start up the bike. I thought, OK he is going to the shop. What transpired was beyond comprehension. The guy took off on the bike at speed around the site like a racing professional. He was scrambling up and down mounds of topsoil. I tried to flag him down and eventually he went to pass the canteen. At this point I stopped him. I gave him an ultimatum. Either get off the bike or get off the site. He nodded as if to conform and then took off like a bat out of hell again, turning the bike into an unfinished driveway and then doing a stunt up a load of stone. The bike went east and he went west. Slamming down on an unfinished stone driveway. No helmet!

I thought the lad is dead. He was lifeless. All the lads from his village that were on the site got up from their tea and started running towards him to assist him. Some were saying, Ah, he has finally killed himself. Then he got up shook his head. Got on the bike, started it and headed for the site entrance. He actually indicated right and took off up the road like there was no limit to the speed the bike could do. The men were disgusted! I thought, Well, that went well. Hard to find labourers and after two hours the only new fellow I could get was gone. Brilliant!

The next week, I kid you not, this fellow arrived on-site posing as a machine driver. Ireland was experiencing something of a boom. There were people chopping and changing jobs in construction on a daily basis. Driven by money and a chronic labour shortage. I had a subcontractor on-site that was supplying heavy equipment such as dump trucks and excavators. He was having similar problems with labour. He was trying to tell me that this fellow had machine driving experience. I point-blank refused to let him on the site. NO! NO! NO! I said angrily. This fella is a fruit and nut. Not a fucking hope. The subbie went against me. I said, Your problem, friend. If he breaks anything you pay! The young fellow was given a 20-ton machine. All sorts of shit could happen. I warned him that I would personally knock seven bells out of him if I ever saw another episode of the week before. Rightly so! I was pent up with rage with the subbie, too. He was between a rock and a hard place. He had a dwindling workforce and a load of work. Fellows like me then roaring for work to be done! Not ideal but that's construction.

Two hours passed. He was charged with the job of filling stone up between the walls inside the house below the floor (rising work). I had this young fellow who was 18 working for me. His job was rolling the stone that the machine was placing in layers with a pedestrian roller. I came to see how they were progressing. I could see that the tops of the walls at floor level were damaged. The blockwork was cracked. I automatically asked the young lad on the roller, why did you break the blockwork? I had warned him about riding the roller too close to the wall. He owned up that it was the Great Bobby G that did the damage. I cleared Bobby the now machine driver away from that job for a moment and sent him up to the rear of the site where he could do no damage. Not so. On his trek up to the back of the site he managed to demolish more blockwork. Two grand in under an hour. I ran him off the job. I lost the plot. I opened the machine door and turned the key and ordered him out. He got out and I locked the door. I walked him to the gate. I warned him to never return again. You are banned. Don't ever let me see you again. I continued: If you see me coming make sure you cross the road. I might not be able to contain myself and give you a clatter.

There was a barring order against him now. Banned? Not Bobby G. Talk about balls! Not a month later this Toyota Dyna van arrived on-site and drove to the house where the block layers were building. I could see in the distance a fellow who seemed familiar. I made my way to that house. When I got close he was taking a bag of tools out of the pick-up. No way, are you staying here. Apparently, he got a job as an apprentice block layer. I warned the subbie. The subbie said that a family member had pleaded with him to give him a job. They were at their wits' end over him. What really got me was the fact that he was smirking at me like, you lost. I was like a lunatic. Within a few hours I was finding walls off plumb which I demolished. Then the subbie fired him a few days later. He couldn't take any more. The last I heard was that he was a roofing contractor in Dublin! You couldn't make it up. I have to hand it to him, he had balls of steel. The guy had no fear. He genuinely didn't give a shit.

Chapter 10

Ireland 1998

CYRIL THE LABOURER. GETTING LIFTED ON
LADIES DAY

Cyril was a fellow of about 50 years old with wispy, light, receding
hair, a thin face, a wispy handlebar moustache and a few red
blotches on his face. I feel he might have been a little fond of
the hard stuff. He was to all intents and purposes a character.
He was a banksman for barbie the crane driver. He, was always
known for the odd bit of skulduggery. A bit of gambling and
possibly more. Who knows? This particular day he got a deal he
didn't bargain for. He decided to go to an exclusive golf club in
an affluent area. He used to frequent this place on a regular basis,
but not as a customer. More as a trespasser. He used to go there
at about 6.30 in the morning of a Sunday and fish around the
lakes for golf balls that were lost during the week. He would then
bag up his finds. On Mondays at lunchtime he would go around
the solicitors' offices and sell them back the balls that they lost
during the week or at the weekend for half the price. A nice
little earner, you would think. He was a sort of wheeler-dealer/
gambler/ducker and diver in his spare time. Always thinking of

how to earn a few quid!

He decided to go out this Sunday morning and while in the lake got caught in a bit of quicksand. This slowed him up for a little while longer. In the interim the ladies were teeing off and they spotted this almost naked, rakishly thin man exiting the lake with only wet Y-Fronts on him. Cut to the next scene. The Gardaí were driving down the fairway at speed with the blue lights flashing. Cyril saw them and decided to make a run for it. He was chased down the fairway by two cops armed with batons and holding onto their Garda hats. He was tackled, manhandled and handcuffed, and then bundled into the back of the squad car while the hoity-toity ladies of society nouveau tut-tutted him. We missed him on Monday. He was charged with indecent exposure and trespass. An expensive collection of balls! That didn't knock even a splinter off the guy. He genuinely didn't give a damn about law and order.

Cyril, overtime and demolition of stone walls, 1994

Our man Cyril worked for another contractor some years earlier. It was the site of a heritage building. The conservation officer had enforced strict rules on the site. All old stone walls had to be removed carefully in order to keep the integrity of the remaining walls and to not cause structural damage to the surrounding buildings. Cyril was removing on average 5 or 6m^2 per day. The contractor was under pressure to get this demolition complete as quick as possible. The new development was behind on its start date. Cyril knew that this foreman was under pressure, call it a sixth sense that the fellow had.

He asked the construction company foreman for overtime at night. The foreman agreed. Time and a half on the money for the extra hours. Cyril went to work that evening on his own. Cyril's plan was to get the walls down as quickly as possible and head home. Call it one hour's work for a four-hour shift.

The foreman arrived the next day to realise that Cyril had demolished 10m^2 of stonework and cleared 3m^2. Half the daytime shift of stone cleared but more demolished. The foreman was suspicious. He asked Cyril to do another double bubble evening shift. Cyril agreed. When Cyril thought everyone was gone home, he got to work. The guy got up on a six-ton dumper and turned down the skip. He then reversed up through the site. Then in position he drove at the wall at speed going down through the gears and hitting the wall at almost full force. He demolished the wall and his career on that job. The foreman lay in wait and immediately broke into an eruption of anger and thus dismissed him. The foreman had been suspicious but never in his wildest thoughts believed that this fellow was so reckless as to navigate a big dumper at speed through an obstructed site and then crash into the walls. Listed walls, for that matter. It might have been to Cyril's advantage that he was sacked. That company folded a few weeks later midway through the project. They were an overextended outfit. Maybe the overtime killed them. Who knows?

Ireland 1998

CYRIL THE LABOURER. CLEARING THE SITE!

Cyril to all intents and purposes was the last of the old Irish characters on construction sites. He was a worker and at times a liability. It was the untold damage that he did that caused controversy. He was a non-conforming type of fellow. The senior engineer and foremen on this particular job tried to fire him a few times. He was responsible for setting the street and a few cars on fire by giving the crane driver the nod to pull a skip up through power lines on the street. Lucky no one was killed. The other thing that Cyril did was fill a 12-yard skip with leftover concrete after a big concrete pour. To add insult to injury he would then put steel in it and then poured more concrete on top of the steel. He had it positioned at the furthest point from the crane. The crane wouldn't be able to lift the load. One might think he did it by design. He might have been having a shot at the crane driver who was trying to get him fired. Who knows!?

The skip was so heavy that the crane couldn't lift it to drop it onto a collection lorry on the street. The neighbouring crane driver on our site had to assist. The two cranes just about lifted it onto the waiting truck and overweight bells on the cranes were wailing. The truck driver was complaining that the truck might buckle under the load. He never saw a skip as heavy. Then again he never met a fellow like Cyril.

Cyril kept the site as clean as a whistle. The area director of the company loved him for that. Any visiting potential client would be very impressed. If a tradesman or labourer left materials, tools or goods in an area and it didn't look tidy enough, Cyril would clear it unannounced. The goods could end up in the skip. One particular day he came across into our site. He asked me could he have four rolls of attic insulation? I gave them to him as refusing could mean more trouble than it was worth.

Then he gave me a piece of paper. Written on it a shopping list of all the items I could have if I wanted them. Lintels, blocks, reinforcing steel and sundry items. Half of their site! I said the reinforcing steel would come in handy as we needed to build four storeys of a stair core in one building. He sent over enough steel for eight storeys. I enquired, Was he sure that they didn't need it? He said he was skipping it. Anyway, fuck 'em, they are not using it and they are leaving the place in shit, was his response! Then the lintels arrived and then new plywood. I had to go into his job and tell him to stop sending stuff over as it was now cluttering up our job. I asked if he wanted it back. He refused and said he was happy.

To this day I firmly believe that he had something on that director. He had him over a barrel on something. Some misdemeanour by the director had caught Cyril's eye. There is no way he would have lasted the duration of any job!

London

THIS

CONSTRUCTION

LIFE...

A series of short stories about my London experiences in a bizarre industry.

Comedy, Construction, Characters.

Chapter 11.

London
LITERALLY.

Things sometimes go tits up! I have to tell it as it is!
The economic crash that took hold of the world in 2007/2008. As I mentioned this led me to seek employment in England. Ireland was literally so damaged economically that I had to go. There was no government subsistence for someone who employed scores of people for years. No, Ireland says no to that! I probably wouldn't have accepted the dole anyway. Many construction people stayed in Ireland. Very qualified construction people in their fifties had to take jobs in factories packing boxes on assembly lines if they were lucky. Working in a factory wasn't me. I was, and still am, a construction man. I packed my bags at 34 years of age and headed for London.

This concept never crossed my mind. I never thought that I would ever emigrate. A far and distant thought for a 14-year-old kid, 20 years earlier watching David and Goliath. If that 14-year-old kid could see me now would he have walked away from construction. We will never know. Shit happened! It sometimes does happen. A couple of right fools caused an economic crash. Then I arrived in London where I discovered an array of both crazy and bohemian people. There were the interesting and extraordinary people, too.

I lived in the early years in England in different places. I lived over a garage and after that in a basement which I didn't like much. It was a tough period. I moved job and then moved to North London. The banks in Ireland wanted to kill me. I was trying to survive under a mountain of debt. It was 2008 and I was leaving Ireland every second weekend to come to England to work. I continued to do this for about five years. Tough wouldn't describe how difficult it was in those few years. I loved having work but travelling every second weekend or every month for a short stay with a pile of debt pressure was not ideal. But I couldn't have lived in Ireland in those years. The pessimism would have killed me. Rising out of bed at 4am to go to the airport for a 6am flight to be on-site at 8.00am on Monday morning was rough at times. It was work, bed, work, bed. I missed life in Ireland but there was no prospect of a return to Ireland. When the economy did finally come around the desire to return subsided.

I was for a while honestly a broken man. Many who did the same stint as me could identify with tough times. I was a site foreman for a naughty Irish subbie. It was challenging, to say the least, with every nationality under the sun and no one could speak English except a digger driver called Gerry from the West of Ireland. A gift from God. I quite honestly cannot fathom how I actually held it together or even remained sane. I suppose that I just immersed myself in work and didn't go home until I was going to bed. It was rough. This leads me on to London characters of Pikies, gangsters and councilmen. It was 2009 and I was working for a construction and civil engineering company in London. We did park refurbishments and groundwork in Central London. This is where I met the council man, the East End gangster and the pikie. "Proper Geezers".

London
PIKIES, GANGSTERS AND COUNCILMEN

Pikies

I was managing a project in East London. We were refurbishing this disused park area. It had a strange-shaped, rectangular mound in the centre of it. First of all, I thought it was an odd-looking mound and questioned it. It didn't belong there. The idea soon left my thoughts. I was busy with getting work done.

We moved into the site. A dilapidated park. We set up a compound and started clearing the park according to our demolition plan. The next day we had excavated concrete and tarmac that had been removed from the old playgrounds. This had to be disposed of off-site. We had this guy, "English Steve", who was our grab lorry driver. He was a cockney geezer with a "fuck off, mate" approach. He never seemed in good form. Otherwise, he was professional in every way. Things had to be done right and he didn't like foreigners. I liked him just for his high standards and knowledge. The foreigners, according to Steve, couldn't do anything right and he let them know in no uncertain terms. They retaliated by making life difficult for him because of his abrasive manner. They mixed all the material which drove him cracked. I was on the upper scale of acceptance. I was Irish. I was a first-class foreigner. I was an acceptable foreigner. We would never be friends but we would be civil to each other.

To return to the pikie story. I left the site to get materials at the builder's merchants. When I returned there was a rusty, old, white box Transit van parked in the entrance to the site. I could see cockney Steve lip reading to me, "fucking pikies". I saw out of the corner of my eye this Whippet of a lad, thin as a lath dressed in runners, tracksuit bottoms and a white T-shirt turning over pallets and rummaging through the rubbish. I walked between the van and the materials, heading for the Whippet. I knew by his physique that he was going to be a tough nut. Harder than a coffin nail by my estimation. Aggressive and non-conforming.

I was passing down the side of the rusty van and then I noticed a fellow in the passenger seat with a big loop earring who was as big as Arnold Schwarzenegger. He glanced at me like a bulldog chewing a wasp. I was not fazed. I made a beeline for this buck who was tearing up the place in search of anything of value. I asked, Who gave you authorisation to enter the site? Fuck off now, boy, while you still got the legs to carry you, he responded. I said, No, you fuck off, boy, and take that big, fat oaf with you. He said, Tell him yourself, boss. He wolf-whistled. The van door opened and like a scene in the film *Snatch* he approached me down the side of this van looking as though he was going to sort me out. The Whippet started telling the oaf, Do ya know what this fella is calling you? He called you a big, fat oaf. He said it in a skit, like Brad Pitt said it in the film *Snatch*. I informed him that he and the big fella were trespassing on our site and I would call the police.

The big fella moved right up close to me, cracking his knuckles and said in a cockney accent, have we a problem, mate?. I knew that it was time to soften. The Whippet said, I am takin' this, boss. It was an old lawn roller made of steel and the wheel was full of concrete. I said that it was worthless and full of concrete but yeah, take it. He said he would paint on some steel colour Hammerite and make it look like steel. 10 out of 10 for his entrepreneurial skills.

The two of them opened the back doors of the rickety, rusty, old van and then I realised that the big fellow was as weak as a lamb. **The big, fat oaf wouldn't kick snow off a rope. Soft as butter.** He had the face of a bulldog and the presence and frame of an evil doorman. A real beauty. Nice Tony, we nicknamed him!

The Whippet looked over at cockney Steve the grab lorry man. He ordered me in his brogue accent to tell that fella with the grab lorry to get over here and give us a hand. I personally wanted this lad off the site. I asked cockney Steve to give them a hand to get the lawn roller in the back of the van. I f***ing hate pikies! he shouted. He reluctantly drove the grab lorry over beside the van. While all this commotion was going on, I could see the big banks of Canary Wharf in the distance. I thought, This is London, right? More like the Wild West!

Steve grabbed the handle of the roller with the grab and started to lift it. The doors of the van were not wrap-around doors so they were open at just over 90 degrees. The "pikie" and the big fella were struggling to pull this lawn roller into the van. The whippet was shouting at cockney Steve, Come on, boss, will you drop it down?! The cockney said, Shut up, mate, I am driving and I am, unlike you, careful. I will do what I like, mate! The pikie kept riling him, Come on will you, you faggot. Drop it, boss? You are holding me up. Now calling cockney Steve a faggot. That's like starting a fight with Phil Mitchell. By this time a crowd of workmen had gathered, including a few Scottish playground installers. Real comedians. They were adding comment to the picture unfolding. In those Scottish Glasgow tones and sniggering they were commenting, "These yer cousins, Paddy, eh?" Steve dropped the grab suddenly. The grab hit the top of the van doors with force and completely bent them.

I nearly burst my sides laughing. The Scots were laughing while hysterically letting expletive after expletive out of their mouths. Everyone was in a flux of laughter. If you laugh that hard sometimes it actually hurts you. That crunch of the grab hitting the doors was an excruciating sound. The men on-site were in bits laughing. The Whippet started into a tirade of abuse at the cockney. He was throwing stuff everywhere. Steve told him to go and f*** off. You told me to drop it, didn't you, mate? No one calls me a faggot, mate. You don't tell me shit, mate! No backing down with Steve. He continued: Who fucking asked you and Fatso to come in here anyway? Did you get lost, mate? The Whippet knew it was a waste of time trying to talk to our Steve. He asked me for some rope to tie up the doors. I had a plastic strap from the pallets that I gave him to tie up the doors.

They eventually left the site after threatening Steve that they would be back for him. Cockney Steve said to me, you need security straight away now, mate. I said Jeez, Steve, did you have to fuck up his van? He retorted proudly, I couldn't give a fuck, mate. Fuck 'em. That "beeeeeeeeeeeeeeep" shouldn't have been in this site anyway. I made that call requesting security on the job. That same afternoon a small, well-spoken East End London geezer dressed in an anorak and jeans arrived. Havin' a spot of bovver, Paddy? Yeah, something like that. No problem, mate. He said in a gravelly accent, I will have a man here at 5 o'clock, mate. Then at 5pm this big, black man called Dr Charles arrived in a big Mercedes. He was imposing-looking but I have to be honest, he wouldn't catch a cold if he had to pursue a thief. I said, This is the site. Can you handle it? YA MAAN, he said in his Nigerian accent. Sorted for another day!

London.

Gangsters

London is laden with these fellows and they are in suits, too. Maybe even banks? Let's not go there! On that particular job we had an Irish machine driver. We will call him John for privacy. John was a West of Ireland man and a damn good machine driver. John was a man in his early sixties and had vices, drink being one of them, and women being the other, as I later learned. John's antics were exposed one day. The company got a new tracker system on all the vans and one day while I was in the head office a young English fellow showed me John's van early in the morning about 4am, leaving his house. Then his van stopped in East London and drove very slowly up and down this road that was known for prostitution. John must have picked up a lady of the night and went to a quiet cul-de-sac in the next street and stayed there for a half-hour before coming to work on a Monday morning of which he arrived in the yard in East London and fell out of the van he was so drunk. When I challenged him that day he told me to Fuck off. I am doing this for 30 years and I am not about to stop now. John was a dinosaur. I had the jobs sheet in front of me and I had more problems than getting into a disagreement at 6.30am on a Monday. When I had my back turned he got into a 7.5-ton truck with a compressor on the back and drove out the gate of the yard like a bat out of hell to the job he was working on. Crazy stuff.

Another foreman challenged him one day and said, you are a washed-up Irish dinosaur. A half-pint! John, being quick-witted, responded, Sure, you are only a broken-down, old ganger man yourself. You will never make foreman! If I was 70 years old like you, I'd call it a day. Might I add that the other foreman who was only about 55 had a slight little drink problem, too! He hid it well.

We were working on the same park with the funny-shaped mound in the middle of the park and the Pikie visit. As part of the contract we had to erect a big £80,000 slide on top of the mound. John the machine driver had started digging the footings for the slide. After a few minutes digging the holes for the feet of this huge slide, he came to the other side of the site to me and said Tyres. I said, John, in English please. I am too busy for your rubbish, John. Fucken' tyres! he responded. Come on, he said in a chipper tone, I will show you.

I walked over to the mound. The two of us looked in the hole and there it was, a big old dumper tyre. I said, Dig the next hole. He did and guess what, more tyres! I was thinking, Lord, how deep are these tyres? We have to erect this slide. We must remove the tyres. There were more tyres and more and more. Now I was worried. I barked, What is this, John? Then John enquired, What is the name of this area again? I reminded him of the name of the road and the park. Ah Jaysus! ... I buried these in the 1970s for an Irish contractor that had to vacate a British Rail yard in a hurry. The story goes that this contractor had to get out of this British Rail yard he was occupying almost 40 years ago.

By now this contractor was a Bentley-driving, pink champagne-drinking, cigar-smoking, respected businessman and used to frequent an East End boozer, parking his Bentley outside the side door where he could keep one eye on it, and the other on the barmaid. Tom, on the other hand, was still a dinosaur, albeit an older one. He got the job of removing those tyres again while Champagne Charlie AKA J.A.Rooney had moved on and made it! He was eyeing a young Barbara Windsor with her assets bursting out through her top in that East End boozer as I one day witnessed.

London

J A Rooney and the East End boozer. This was the pub scene
John A. Rooney was a native of County Mayo in Ireland. He was a civil engineering contractor in London's East End. He done well. I didn't know much about this fellow only that I saw his signs everywhere on the roads in East London and his tipper lorries were everywhere, too! He was a rival of the guy I worked for at the time. He was the guy who buried the tyres in the East London park in the 1970s. He was always suited and booted and used to drink in a pub called the George. Pinstriped suits and pink champagne, no less! The pub used to stock it especially for him. Our lads knew him. He drove a Bentley and parked it at the side door of the pub. One Friday after work and months of refusing the guys who worked for me, I gave in to their demands of going for a drink with them after work.

The gg's were on the telly. J Rooney all dressed up, having his flute of pink shampoo and dressed in a three-piece suit. One eye on the Bentley and the other on the staff. Del, Triggs and Rodney were outside the counter with their tartan flat caps and their woodcock mannerisms. All a bit dodgy. Selling counterfeit goods to one another and having a flutter on the gg's. This was their manor.

An illegal gambling room at the back of the pub. Stacks of money visible when the door rarely opened. A cigar-smoking bulldog behind the desk of the gambling room and a couple of phones in front of him. Peggy Mitchell, a young, attractive Barbara Windsor bird with her high stilettos, peroxide blonde hair and her assets, bursting out of her tight top as she threw out the pints to the boys.

More like the Queen Vic than the George. She possessed a real East End attitude. Nice but naughty. I'd say if you caught her eye then you were in danger. Abrasive, to say the least. She was tough. Any trouble and she would have your hand halfway up your back and your head would be used as a battering ram to breach the door. The Albanians, Moldovans, Romanians and Bosnians would shout up their orders, in a raised tone. Two more pints, darling, and she would be down their throats shouting the odds that she would be clearing them if there was another outburst.

This lad Baghir was a tough nut. Once you corrected him he would go off on one. That is when about three of us put our hands over his mouth. We wanted a quiet pint.

As I surveyed the pub, this is what I saw. Del, Triggs and Rodders were all turned and looking in our direction, sizing us up. There was a baldy fellow in the corner who was probably security. Not the place for a row, even though I would say that the lads I was with would break the place up with ease.

Two pints and that was it. I was out of there before the glasses started flying and biddies were crying. It was an East End scene in a glass time capsule. The underworld gambling was in full fettle. Not many of them boozers left now. A real atmosphere of a bit of banter, sticky carpet, dowdy 70s wallpaper and, ahem, gambling.

London

The Councilman...

I was in London only a few months and was still gathering myself and meeting a completely different set of rules head on. Bad enough that I met the pikies and John, but then I met this councilman. He appeared a posh fellow! He was impeccably turned out with his crisp, white shirt, grey slacks, sensible loafers and a red tweed tie in a basic knot. He handed me the plans and told me in an old school headmaster's authoritative tone that he would return tomorrow to see how I was performing. I felt that I was about to sit an exam. The next morning me and the crew, mostly Eastern Europeans and Albanians, arrived for work. As any good foreman would, I put them to work on the park demolition. I was working like I did in Ireland with enthusiasm.

Then at 10am the posh councilman arrived. He enquired in a troubled tone, Oh my word, what are you doing? I told him I was following the plans. Put them away, he said crossly. He uttered, Tut-tut. Let's take a walk in the park. The gauche councilman would tell me to scrap all the information on the plans and then proceeded to tell me that I was only to carry out certain works. What a generous guy! I wondered why. Well, someone let it slip sometime later. True or not we will never know. It turns out that this guy caused the contractor untold financial losses some years earlier and in the interim he was maybe feeling guilty or maybe he was visited by a man with a bag in the middle of the night. Who really knows? To make amends he just corruptly wanted to let the contractor do the bare minimum work. He was a real gentrified sort of chap. He used to refer to me in Queen's English accent as Mr B. Never as my Christian name. I always called him Mister, too!

Then he was landed with the understudy. I could tell he was not happy with the fact that this lady was with him. She would never really get to know him. God bless her, she was too green. He would arrive on the job with his understudy tottering along behind him. A pretty, young, 20-something Polish architect. A very nice girl. Totally oblivious to what this guy was really like. He would tell her to go and take a load of photos for the archive. Long-distance ones just in case his game would be up. Clever bastard! Then he would proceed to cut down on the works. Leave that out and don't do this. I protested. He ignored!

The young lady would arrive back after her photography jaunt to be told that he was leaving. Now come along, young lady, let's not keep Mr B any longer. I am sure he has a lot to be getting on with. No, not really, I thought. You just made sure I had less to do. He would then throw in a comment that he is not happy with something and that I was to rectify it before his next visit. I would always say, Yes, of course. What a fraud! I needed the job and the money. I was, after all, an immigrant and I was after taking a huge fall after the financial meltdown. He would say things like, we ordered ten benches for this park but I rather think that nine will suffice. Then he would ask if the company had any vans with no signwriting on them. Then he would complement two or three workmen on the site. Then he would say, Put the spare bench somewhere safe.

I agreed. Then he would enquire was I the reading type? Then he would erupt into praise for his lovely wife, "er indoors", and say how she was an avid reader in the summer in the garden. The seat she uses is a bit tired now and it doesn't bear much of a relationship to the order of the garden. These benches, however, are very nice, he would continue. I had no doubt about what I needed to do. I just came out with it: Do you want it put into your garden?

There I had it: the boys he praised were to bring the bench to his house in a plain van with no signwriting and install the bench in his back garden at some date yet to be decided. I awaited instruction. I decided to say a few things one day to a contract manager when he was showing me a new project. I said to our boy that this council guy, let's call him Tony Soprano, was a very nice guy. It was like *The Italian Job*. I didn't get a response from this fellow. He just looked away and said nothing. I then knew this kind of stuff was most definitely the norm in London. Fair enough.

The final straw for me was when I was completing a park in London not far from where the Krays used to hang out. There were benches and bins to be installed as the last job to complete our works in this park. There was a lady living nearby who was a member of the local committee. She was always interfering and a bit of a ranter but then I had been warned about her by yours truly from the start. I used to let her rant and rave. She did a lot of that. I used to diffuse her by speaking well and just being polite. It worked! This lady was always on about seeing the drawings. I was told at the start of the project by Tony Soprano, she is not to be shown any drawings at any time. In the end Tony and I were in the park and she appeared. Then she was calling Tony to ask him about the location of the benches. He said to me, pretend you didn't hear her. Let's walk away over here to the other side of the park. Muttering, that wretched woman. A real pain in the posterior.

We waited for her to go away and then he told me where to put the benches and bins – but do not spray anything on the ground as a marker, he authorised. I put twigs on the ground so I would remember the location.

In the end she waited like a lion in the long grass for him to get close to her flat and then she pounced. He was caught. He had to speak to her.

Well, then, she enquired, where are these benches and bins going? He had just told me. She was concerned because the drug dealers used to hang out on the benches and she didn't want them near her house. But it was alright if it was in front of someone else's home. He responded to her in his very posh accent that he needed to ask what the board's decision was on it. He would probably know in a few weeks! What a load of bollocks. We walked away. Not a word, he uttered. Wait till she is out, have the men nearby and install them. Get them all in and be gone, were his instructions!

That was when I realised that I needed to get out of there myself. "That's London and the characters you meet"!

Chapter 12

London

LONDON CHARACTERS

The site Characters I met from my early days in London!
Eddie the Albanian AKA "Porn Star Eddie"
Eddie was Baghir's Albanian cousin. You will learn all about Baghir later. Eddie, like Baghir, had that tough warrior look. Most of them Albanians have that defined jawline. He had cropped blond hair and the cut of a tough man. He was as mad as a box of frogs. He always approached you with a smile but don't be lured into a false sense of security by that smile. He had a very short fuse and he could beat you up if he lost the rag with you. If you riled him it was at your peril. These boys had a hard life. Their existence was just an existence.

Eddie left Albania and stowed away up through Europe, starting off as a farm labourer in Greece. He didn't like the Italians and so he kept going until he got to France. He maintained that the Italians were a mean-spirited bunch. But then he might have been up to mischief. He got into trouble with the Gendarmerie in Paris. He told me he got caught selling hash in the park in Paris for a distant cousin. My brother, who was working for me at the time, told me that story on the way home from work on a foul, wet January evening. That was the thing about Eddie. He was a bit innocent and certainly had no filter. He could say anything. You would have to know how to navigate situations with him when he got out of hand.

Back to Paris. The Gendarmerie locked him up for two weeks. Then one day they left him out of the cells. They gave him all his belongings and drove him to the countryside north of Paris. They gave him some money and told him he had two weeks to leave the country. They warned him if they saw him ever again, they would send him down for a minimum of two years. They advised him of his options. There were two. You can go to Italy but the Italian border police are too clever and will not let you back into Italy. England is that way, and that is easy. Off you go. Don't let us see you again. He got it.

He was heading to Calais anyway before he was caught selling hash in the park! I suppose he needed the money. Eddie's uncle and cousin were in London anyway. He arrived at the port in France and waited for Albanian-registered lorries and picked one and strapped himself to the underside of an artic trailer. He arrived in Dover and nearly got caught by the sniffer dogs. He admitted to me that he was quite scared of getting caught when he could see the border guard and the dogs' legs. He maintained that the night was so cold that the dogs' nasal passages were blocked and that is why the dogs didn't detect him. Once the truck stopped a few miles from the port he unstrapped himself and absconded into the countryside in search of London without a rasp of English. I suppose that is the life of an illegal immigrant.

He was a prolific worker and quite artistic. He told me that when children are a year old in Albania their mothers used to bring them to the sea and throw them into the water. Only when they were about to drown would they remove them from the water. The same ritual would be practised the next day until they could swim. This was supposed to strengthen their character. It certainly did make them strong characters. I can safely say they are always ready to fight and don't like authority. They are, on the other hand, very diligent and honest workers. I say that with truth.

Eddie was a colourful chap. Diligent, hard-working and seriously artistic. He used to do tattoos in his spare time. He had an eagle on his chest. He had a penchant for women. He absolutely loved women and had about three girlfriends. He was short in height but he could get a girl's attention. I think it was the tiger smile. His phone would be ringing in the morning from the time we collected him in the yard to the time we dropped him back in the evening. I would enquire, do you want to answer that call, Eddie? No, would be his response. I don't like that lady anymore. He used to call them ladies.

Eddie had no filter on his vocabulary

Eddie had no filter. One morning I was going to work and his phone was ringing and I asked, How many girlfriends have you now, Eddie? I have lots of ladies, he responded. But at the moment I have three ladies. I have an 18-year-old, a 25-year-old and a 33-year-old. He said, I don't like the 25-year-old lady. She was probably on to him anyway. I really like the 33-year-old lady, she has big tits, and he was smiling with enthusiasm. He made it sound like it was a continent that he was describing. I really like the 18-year-old lady, he continued, but she smokes cannabis. I don't like that. Then the bombshell arrived. All this time he was smiling into his Nokia phone and there it was, he said it. Laughing and talking at the same time: This is me last night washing her in the bath. I nearly crashed the van. I said, Jaysus, Eddie, that is private stuff. The men in the back were saying, He is at it again. Some guy from Bosnia piped up and passionately lambasted him: You are fucking crazy, man. He just laughed. It went straight over his head. He found a picture of himself and the girl – with clothes on, I might add, in the photo – smiling.

OK. Ed, put away the phone. Why, Paddy? he responded. I just said, Give it up, Eddie. That was the thing: nothing was private with him and he would say things to officials or high-ranking people if he felt the need. Things like you don't know how to design parks to a designer. But when he gave his advice, he would have thought it out. It would be an intelligent proposal. It was weird. He was, though, a crazy bastard.

I would then have to apologise to the official after he was gone. Making excuses for him by saying he suffers from a mental disorder but we have to keep him. He is our token worker. A new government incentive. Pure shite but it worked!

London

Eddie the Albanian and the Woolwich Job incidents.
The black man was on Eddie's radar!

One time we were doing a job on a big roundabout in Woolwich Arsenal in East London. There was me and a gang of about four men, including Eddie. Out of nowhere this black man who had his shirt off and was completely strung out on drugs walked across two lanes of oncoming traffic on this busy road. He started trying to carjack some cars. He was stopping the cars and then trying to open the driver's door. In a few attempts he tried to break the windows with his fist. Most cars were just swerving around the guy and driving on again.

We watched intently, knowing that we would all make a move on him if he succeeded. But there was Eddie. In true Albanian spirit he picked up a coal shovel and jumped out over the steel barrier by the roundabout. He started shouting, I am going to hit him over the head! He was taking stork steps at first and then he flew into a sprint. We started calling him to return back to work. The black fellow saw him coming. His eyes nearly fell out of his head with fright seeing this fellow in hi-visibility clothes coming at him, roaring in Albanian that he was going to knock him out with the shovel. The black lad started running and then thought he might get cheeky and hurl abuse at Eddie. No, not a good idea. Then Eddie started to close ground on him so he shut up and fucked off. Eddie was not a guy to give up. He was a terrier when he got something in his head. A good lesson for a carjacker – please be sure Eddie the

Albanian is not around when you decide to carjack in broad daylight. Beware of the consequences. He didn't catch that fellow. LUCKY GUY.

The girlfriend arrives

On a fabulous summer's day on that very same job, Porn Star Eddie announced one day smiling and excited that his girlfriend was coming to see him. The guy was jumping up and down like an elated child in a sweetshop. I could see our machine driver who was 60 years old and from Fermanagh in Ireland roll his eyes and sigh, Oh Jaysus, in true Irish style. Then he pursed his lips and shook his head and quipped, For fuck's sake, Eddie.

About 15 minutes passed and Eddie started to get more excited. She is coming, she is coming. LOOK! LOOK! This young, 20-something girl was confidently walking towards us. She had these tight hot pants on her and a boob tube top and the boobies were well, very much out. More out than in if you know what I mean. She was wearing modern Amy Winehouse boot shoes, laces open and all. She was a cocky sort of girl. I would say attention-seeking and possibly a screw loose, too! All the men stood and drooled as this bird made her way down the street to where we were working. She approached the temporary pedestrian orange barrier and Eddie like a child ran up the inside of the barrier to meet her. She nearly sucked the face off him as she snogged his face off ferociously. He was about 5ft 5 in height and she was 6ft 2. Very funny. She was definitely in control. She then looked at the men and then they both fell over into the site with the barriers between them. The whole length of barriers went over. I walked over and said, Eddie, go on, bring her home or get a room or something. This is not good enough. Get out of here. He turned to me giggling like a child and said, Isn't she nice? (he used to pronounce the word 'nice' as 'no ice'). I said, Yes, she is, now go. He said, Come on, we will go for coffee. 'Cwuoffee'. Eddie, I said, go home. As I turned to the other men, they were all in stitches and doubled over laughing. Everyone laughed for a few minutes. That's why he was called Porn Star Eddie. You couldn't make this stuff up!

London
BAGHIR THE ALBANIAN

Baghir was an excellent and most prolific worker. He was also Porn Star Eddie's cousin. He came to England from Albania when he was 14 years old. He stowed away all the way up through Europe, starting in Greece. He crossed the English Channel on a ferry as a foot passenger. How he got through Customs was genius for a 14-year-old kid. He filed in behind a family with four children and had a sunhat on him. He had long, blond hair and the border police must have thought he was a little girl. The border guard just waved him on with the family.

He headed to London where his Uncle Sen was living. When he arrived in London it was to Mile End. There was a contractor working in the park. An Irish fellow by the name of Jonny Horan. Jonny was a bit of a naughty boy, too. A drinker, a carouser and a bit of a lairy gangster. Anyway, this kid asked him through the fence, Hey, mister, any chance of a job? The kid, remember, had long hair. The Irish guy asked in his gravelly Irish accent, Are ya a boy or a girl? The kid got offended and shouted, I'm a boy man!

The Paddy then growled, cut your hair and come back tomorrow and I will give you a job. Sure enough, the kid arrived the next day at 7am ready for work. Well, the rest is history. Paddy put the young teenager to work. He was very good at digging and a real smart kid. He was hired.

Baghir was as thin as a lath. He was hard-looking. Seychelles blue eyes and high cheekbones. A little bit of a gypsy cut, if I am being honest. He had a short fuse and he definitely suffered from ADHD attention deficit. He sometimes had that vacant look in his eyes when the mind was taxed a bit. He was into all sorts of vices. Gambling habits being one.

These guys were exposed to far too much stuff and possibly hardship of some sorts early in life. No home, no job, no family, travelling on your own. This could be disorientating and scary. Many traps and unscrupulous people on the way. Life in Albania was hard for them. Not ever seeing your family again once you left home was a normal phenomenon. 20 years after leaving Albania as a 14-year-old he returned as a British citizen to visit his father just before he died.

The guy had some physique. A washboard of a stomach. 12 pack. He would strip off his T-shirt on a hot summer's day and women would be leering at him from afar. He eventually met this nice Indian woman and we thought that she would be a great influence on him. The boss asked him one day how was the girl. He said in his Albanian accent, I got rid of her, she smelled too much like curry!

The deal was, the boss used to pay him a third of his wage weekly and hold the rest in an account until a holiday period. Otherwise he would spend it all on a Friday night in the gambling establishments around Bethnal Green in East London.

Baghir saved my bacon once from an absolute lunatic when we were refurbishing a park in Peckham. I hear you say Peckham. Yes, Del Boy country… I will be always eternally grateful to him for this one.

This big, black guy parked up in a car park near our job. We had our site cordoned off with steel Heras fencing in order to protect the site and the public. This guy walked up to the fence and ripped the fence apart in front of me, breaking steel clips that were doubled up. He was heading for a crèche. Now the fence was double-clipped. He was definitely stronger than normal. I thought you could only achieve this if you were on some sort of stimulant.

I was having my break. I absolutely lost it and started roaring at this guy to get out of our job and he will have to pay for the damage. He told me, Shut the fuck up, and reminded me he would do what he liked. He proceeded to the other side of the job and broke two more fence panels. I just followed and put the fences back together and clipped them back up. The guy was back ten minutes later and fucked up four more panels. I was like a dog.

He told me he would be back to fuck me up. I shook my

head in disbelief. WTF! I proceeded to watch him return to his van in the car park. It was a white escort van. He opened the back door of it. Then he emerged with what looked like a long-shanked screwdriver and was making a beeline for me.

It was a hot summer's day and the Albanians and Bosnians were taking shade under a tree. Baghir, Sem, Jon (Magore), Baz and a few Romanians, too! I started to make my way over to my lads. When the black man approached the fence he was spitting fire and threatening how he was going to kill me. They guy was completely out of it on drugs and frothing at the mouth. I was nervous, to be honest. I had told Baghir I was in bother with this lad before he came to the fence. No bother, Paddy, he responded we saw everything. I can handle him.

When this guy came to the fence shouting at me, Baghir and the gang of men jumped up like a pack of hounds. This didn't frighten the black man at first. He was still raving. The next thing Baghir started opening the clips on the fence. He said, Come in, man. But if you come in you will not leave. The black fellow backed down. He was still mouthing off but you could see it in his eyes: he went from aggressive to frightened. I was happy, though. He got a taste of his own medicine. I went to the reception in the crèche as I thought, what destruction did he do there? The lady at the desk said the police were called and there was an order against him to keep away. He apparently caused absolute consternation there, too! Family issues…

He didn't bank on meeting Baghir!

Chapter 13

London

STARTING MY BUSINESS IN LONDON. GRAND
THEFT AUTO!

*My grandfather had a saying: the old dog for the hard road,
the pup for the path.*
I got the hard road. They say Frankie went to Hollywood.
Paddy went to Cricklewood! All the shit happened here!
It was the year 2011. I had my fill of the frantic life running
sites for high-rise concrete frame construction companies.
Four hours' sleep a night. My monthly bank debts in Ireland
were not getting any better. I needed to get my hands on more
money. I decided after almost three years working for other
people in London to start my own company. I hadn't a brass
tack to my name. But in true Irish brazen style, I decided to
start a company. Just to make it easy a "construction company"
in a recession time! I was a headbanger by any standards. I just
wanted to earn more money to solve my problems. I had no
work and three weeks to go in my job.

My employer was laughing at the prospect and asking,
have you got work? I brazenly said, No! Ah sure, won't it be

grand Irish style. I will have a cup of tea and think about it. I was panicking a bit if I am honest. For the last two weeks of employment I started doing work in the evenings and over the weekend to get my hands on some money. Moonlighting. I would do anything to get a few quid in the coffers. It was tough. One day out of the blue a contractor I knew called me and asked me was I busy? I returned that I was now a subbie (subcontractor) and I was interested in taking on projects that would be funded by him. If he kept the payments coming. I could do the work and deal with the architects and any professionals. He would have little to do! The rates for the men were agreed. We had bonus-related targets, too! That was a great catalyst to gain ground, buy vans and tools. We were all set. It was a park refurbishment in Chelsea. If I knew then what I was about to learn I don't think I would have had the stomach for it.

I started the job on a Tuesday morning. The normal procedures applied. Fence off the site. Get the machinery and office in a compound. We are ready to start the demolition. I brought two of my brother's friends from Ireland to London to work for me. The economy in Ireland was in an absolute diabolical state. No jobs in construction whatsoever. High unemployment. A basket case of an economy! They came willingly but were shocked by the pace and harsh lifestyle here. Things were tough here, too! Prices and wages were tight. Anyway, I used to collect these boys in the morning and bring them to work in a Pajero SUV which I was returning to Ireland soon. I had got a loan from a friend and purchased a white

Mercedes sprinter van. That Pajero was stolen on Friday off the job when we turned our back for five minutes. The Irish machine driver moved my jeep out of the way of some work. He failed to realise that you need to lock everything in London. It had in it all my engineering equipment, my passport, driving licence and some dockets with the address of where I lived. I was heading to the boat that Friday to leave that jeep in Ireland after all! I jumped into the pick-up truck we had on-site and raced down streets in Sands End near Battersea Bridge. Driving down backstreets near the river into underground car parks, into council estates trying to see if I could find where it was hidden. They would have to dump it quick so it wasn't detected by the authorities.

I called the police. That was as effective as pissing into a gale coming in off the Atlantic. Filled out some forms and the questionnaires. I have great respect for the police. It is not the police's fault that these bastards got out of bed that morning. The cops have bigger fish to fry!

I licked my wounds over the weekend. I felt a bit low, to be honest. But hey, I have a job to do so get on with it. I drove the white van I just bought to work on Monday morning. This was a replacement for the SUV that I was returning to Ireland. I collected the two boys on Monday morning from the flat they were living in, in Willesden Green. I was paying £140 per week each for them to share a rat-infested room on the third floor of this building.

I just got on with the work. By Wednesday of that week I was feeling better. It did strike me that there were many undesirables walking around the park and watching us. I did get the sixth sense that we were under surveillance. There were lads walking a British bulldog with a different coloured patch on one eye. The dog was the same but the people changed. They were also smoking weed. The stink off that stuff. Come Thursday I went home after work. Dropped off the boys and went home to my house. It was September and it was dark at about 9pm. I remember parking the van and the back wheel was touching the kerb. I looked out of the glass door in the porch and thought I should have parked that better. The van was nicked that night.

I woke at 5.30am the next morning and went out of the door. No van. I thought I was dreaming. I walked back inside, looked at my watch and looked up the stairs. No, it's not a dream! Definitely I am awake! I called the police. I made a statement that evening. I had an old banger of a Jag parked down the road. I went to work that morning in the Jag. I was paranoid at this stage. After the two vehicles were nicked, I used to park my Jag about a mile from where I lived. I would take different routes home in order to evade any possible tail by these guys. They never got the chance to steal the Jag. I am convinced that it was because I used to hide it.

At this point it was clear to me we had enemies from some quarter. I asked a few neighbours near the jobsite discreetly, what was I missing? One brave working-class guy more or less told me that there were drug dealers living on the 17th floor of a council block. They were trying to break me. I was renovating a park that they were doing their regular trade in. How was I to know? I have a feeling that everyone in the locality knew the guys were responsible for what happened. Nobody would talk here as this gang was intimidating the community. There was worse to come!

The next weekend came around. On the Monday that followed I opened the gates into the job to be exposed to a circus of a site. The place was absolutely destroyed. All the machinery was absolutely fucked. No windows in the machinery. All the consoles of the machinery were totally destroyed. The banger of a Transit tipper pick-up had no windows. The place looked like a war-torn country. I was totally deflated. These drug lords paid all the naughty kids in the area a fiver to completely destroy the machines. They did an exceptional job. Welcome to London, Paddy! I was going to cancel the 30 cubic metres of concrete that we were going to pour that morning.

I genuinely didn't know where to go with this. Not only was I an immigrant that had suffered a heavy fall from the economic crash of 2007, but I was also living in another country with no money, social life or family, and these guys were trying to kill me, too! I didn't know who was worse, the banks or the drug dealers. I had had enough. I was striving to get back on my feet. I was being belted into a corner by these bastards. I was on the verge of tears when, Porn Star Eddie came to the rescue. He said, Hey, Paddy boy, what's wrong with you, man. Let the concrete come. I will have them machines moving in a few minutes. He joined up wires that he picked up from around the site and one by one started all the machinery. Now, I might add he nearly electrocuted himself a few times by putting a copper pipe on the starter motor to shock the electrical coil into motion. He maintained that once you get a diesel engine turned on it will stay on. I used to fix machinery without the computer technology. Eddie knew how to bypass all this as a result of his Army training. Eddie served two years' national service in the Albanian Army. An electronics specialist and tank operator. I had the pleasure of being a work colleague of this guy. There was nothing this fellow didn't know.

Grand Theft Auto

The Army in Albania wasn't exactly a friendly place. He was honoured as a model soldier and was hand-picked after completing his national service as an aid to the president of Albania in the capital Tirana. With Eddie's help, we poured the concrete that day.

Later, the weather started to get cold and we had to collect small batches of concrete for placing concrete kerbs etc... I had to get into that van with no windows and drive to the concrete plant. I used to put on a second coat and drive the van down the backstreets to the concrete plant with Oasis up full pelt on the CD player to keep sane. It would be raining hard on me in the van on the way to collect it.

The main contractor was a very decent fellow. I was on the point of failure. I lost all my tools, two vans, and hadn't an arse in my trousers: he offered me the loan of a van. He asked me to take the worst van in his yard. We took one that had big dents in it. We were on-site the following week and hey presto, they struck again. In broad daylight a shiny black Volkswagen

Transporter van reversed into the site at speed. The side door opened in front of us. A heavy-set man with a balaclava and a baseball bat got out of the van and ripped into the windows. All the men on the job, fair play to them, ran at this fellow. The guy was being roared at by his accomplices in the van to C'mon, c'mon, let's get out of here or they will get you. His malicious attack was getting the better of him and he was staying to get the last smash in.

The van started revving and started to move and they sped out of there with that bastard halfway in the van with his baseball bat dragging along the tarmac. I was worried now. I thought these boys will shoot us next. I asked the police for some sort of protection. They used to patrol the park in the middle of the day after I complained to the council in writing. This took the heat off us during the day. These boys were up to a lot. They were playing a game with us hard-working slaves from Ireland. We hadn't a bean and we didn't deserve such abuse.

I was thinking of going to Australia. I am here almost three years and then I start a company and then a crowd of degenerates are trying to sink me. I was thinking there must be a sunnier place. It was tough. I survived that one, though. I am still here to tell the tale. I had toyed with going for a drink but I thought that I might not have stopped in my state of mind! Plenty of lads there crying into their pints! That was not going to be me.

A year passed and the lady from the council who was a New Zealand citizen called me out of the blue to tell me that there was a sting operation on those thugs. They were all jailed. Looking for my van and jeep would have jeopardised the operation. I was probably not helping the situation by having a go at them! But, thinking back, we never saw any police there until I asked them to patrol the park. Before we completed that park regeneration they hit me one more time.

I was doing a private refurbishment for another client at the same time I was doing this park refurbishment. He insisted that he paid me some money on a Friday evening as an interim payment. The job was almost complete. I met him in a pub in North London. One of those big Victorian pubs with big, ornate windows. I met him and collected the envelope of cash. It was to be banked the next morning. The company really needed the money. It was teetering above the line. On my way home from collecting the cash payment I got a sixth sense. I had a thought that I needed to hide the money when I got home. Now ten grand takes a good bit of hiding in a small room. I decided to hide it in pairs of socks. The sense was so strong I stuck an envelope to the back of the chest of drawers. If anyone pulled the drawers they wouldn't suspect that there was money strapped to the unit. Real effort! I even stuck a few notes up behind the radiator from the bottom. Who would look there? I thought.

I left the house and went for a bite to eat. I returned two hours later. There was a police car outside the house and two police officers in the hall. The landlady who, God bless her, was an older woman was crying in the hall. The kitchen window was broken and there was glass all over the kitchen. I asked the police could I enter my room to see if there was anything gone. I entered my bedroom: it was totalled. Absolutely wrecked. I just went for the socks that were all over the room. Oh! Yes, money there. OK. Radiator. Result! Drawer unit. Still there. Not one penny did those bastards get. They took a computer and some change. Somebody from above was praying for me. That would most certainly have sunk me. The little feckers did take some jewellery from the old lady. She didn't deserve it. I gave the police a statement. Never heard another thing about it.

I found out that I was now working harder with the added pressure of paying about 40 men. I had no loans or overdrafts with banks. It was money in and money out. If I didn't have the money I would be f***ed. Real pressure! I knew that this was going to be hard. It was. I remember one night pulling up at a red light in my van at King's Cross station and I saw these young revellers falling out of a nightclub. It was 2.30am on Saturday morning and I had been up since 4am on Friday morning. That's how hard I was working to keep the whole thing going. I suppose it takes either resilience or madness to continue when this sort of stuff is happening. A good lesson in life for anyone who wants a taste of the dark side. Don't try this at home. You must be in London to get the full effects of such an experience.

Chapter 14

London
ADAM AKA ARFUR DALEY

The name Arthur Daley refers to a TV character from English television in the 70s and 80s. A sort of underworld businessman. A Jaguar-driving, cigar-smoking ducker and diver from London. I have spelled the name Arthur 'Arfur', as it would be pronounced in London. The thing about being a small subbie in London is that getting a yard space to rent is like trying to find a needle in a haystack. There are hundreds of thousands of people just like you looking for the same thing. The London geezer will be trying to get a premium for a less than favourable yard. Yard space was, and still is, scarce. Hen's teeth. Every square inch of space is being developed into apartments.

When I started a business in London in 2011 money was scarce. I rented a yard from a London geezer called Adam, or Daley as I used to call him. He used to say, Awright, Butler, and chuckle in a loud East End London laugh. He would make fun of me, comparing me to a streak of misery character called Butler on the 1970s TV series, *On the Buses*. He thought it was funny; I didn't. £800 per month, boy! That's what the yard is going to cost you. For a pile of shite, I responded. Look, Pat, he would respond, they are queuing up, mate. He would be a guy to be having a laugh and then you would mention something about money and his eyes and face would change to that of a lion! Focused...

Daley thought a month was 28 days. He was a "proper gangster". Harder than stone. He always had another underhand motive to extract more money from you. Just to let anyone who is unfamiliar with London money slang know, a score is a £20, a pony is a £50, a ton is £100, a monkey is £500 and the slang "bees and honey" means money.

Daley had no scruples, possibly because he was dealing with rough diamonds on the ground. He was the son of a fruit vendor. This fella could count. He was streetwise, smart and abrasive if you were out of favour with him. In England we would call him an arrogant sort! In Ireland we would call him a bollix. I would safely say that he would always add up things to suit himself. A skinflint. He had bother with the ex-wife. Not a happy camper. I could imagine this guy staring at the ceiling at 4 in the morning plotting who he was going to hit today for more money. One morning I was in this yard I was renting from him in North London. I was collecting my mail off Fran, the gateman. Fran was alright. He worked for Daley for years. He was a decent guy. Daley was sitting at the main desk opposite Fran and in his London geezer loud voice was talking and chuckling. Enough to put you off your cornflakes!

Willie, who was a big Irish subcontractor, walked into

the gate lodge to hang up his keys from his own yard. Daley boomed, Good morning, Willie, and how are you on this fine summer's morning? Willie barked back in his less than amused Irish accent, what's good about it? Willie immediately fucked off after making the comment. Daley said to me, What a rude man, Pat. He continued. I believe it's nice to be nice, Pat. Daley had a different idea of what the word 'nice' meant. Willie knew more than me about this fellow! I was only around a short while. He had met a few Daleys before! I found out later that Willie was a decent chap but he knew Daley better than I did. He was setting the trend for Daley. If Willie was friendly, Daley would think this guy is easy, let's kick his head in for more money on the rent. Daley knew Willie was a big subbie and he had money.

Adam AKA Arfur Daley and having the poor mouth

I very quickly learned that you didn't show Daley any hint that you were making money. No new vans, no new cars. If he asked you, how was business, you told him, "It's a bit slow at the moment." Like you were a poor West of Ireland farmer. If you were doing well, Daley would resort to telling you that he needed a yard for a fellow he couldn't place. He would then ask you if you needed all that space. Even though I left that yard early in the morning and didn't come back sometimes till late in the evening, you would see that fellow five times in five days. He was like a bad penny. The thing about all this was that I was a decent sort that expected fairness. But this didn't exist here. I copped on quick!

On his question about the yard, the clever response would be to say, Leave it with me. Then be scarce around the place. He would forget because he had other problems. There were plenty of naughty fellows in his yards who wanted to break his balls. There were plenty of fellows that attracted the Old Bill. Not that this bothered him one bit. This kind of stuff gave Daley a busy day every day. I could quietly get on with my business and he wouldn't bother me much.

The thing about him was you didn't ask him for anything. The toilets were barely functioning and you would need a boat to get to my yard space in wet weather. There were lakes of water about 3ft deep in places. If you complained, you were in the line of fire for a request for more money. If you complained too much, he would get narky and try to get you out of the yard. I really needed the yard so I kept quiet. His form of defence would always resort to saying, Will you get lost? You are lucky to have a yard. He was a prick of the highest order. I often thought to ask him what was the difference between the fellow inside a white pick-up and a hedgehog.

Some people just have a rough disposition built into them. This fellow was definitely one of them.

Chapter 15

London

PADDY AND THE BANK OF ENGLAND SAFES

I know what you are thinking. The title suggests some sort of skulduggery. You would be right! It involved just a few Paddys. A few bold boys. After a hard work week in London as usual. Round-the-clock stuff. One Friday night I decided to go for a pint in Neasden. I used to stay out of Irish pubs if I could at all. This Friday I just felt like a pint. In a big economy with a large population you do find a few more fruit cakes.

In this case, the fruit and nut was Irish. So, there I was on Friday night at about 9 o'clock in the pub having a quiet pint in north London, and then this Irish lad from Co. Kerry started quizzing me. Well, boy, where are you from? I responded, Limerick. Kerry, he responded. Are ya in construction? Who do ya work for? Yes, I work for myself. Oh ya. What do ya do? Groundwork and light civil engineering. What's with the questions? I then returned the questions. Are you a guard? What do you do? Oh, I am a plasterer. Anyway, I got the story. He was a plastering contractor in Chicago and was in business with another fellow. He got a lot of work from the gay community. Good for him. He did well. He was married and had a son with an American woman. All was going well – except!

He, to say the least, was "a naughty boy". He would receive a big lump of money into his account on a Friday night from a wealthy client. Then he would get a last-minute flight to Vegas for a weekend of drunken debauchery with his friend/business partner. Wolf of Wall Street stuff! Now separated from the American wife and a ten-year-old son in Chicago. Things sometimes go wrong! He might have helped.

He is lamping the pints in front of me in a pub in Neasden. A pub I never frequented again. He tells me that he had to bail out of America. The father was sick in Ireland and then he died. I had to go home, he exhaled. He didn't get on with the mother, brother or granny. Land issues. The farm was split up into two parts. Family problems how are you. I knew that there was some story coming. He broke into a story about his current employer going on holidays and he was running out of work for him! I knew that this fellow was not giving me the full SP. He continued that his current employer was a bit of a bollix or so he maintained. I felt there was more to this Paddy! Drink may have been his God.

His current boss was a fellow from Belfast no less. He continued that your man had a lovely wife and he used to cheat on her with prostitutes that used to rent a building from him. They used to take the service off the rent! I think Paddy used to frequent the same establishment! No actually I'm pretty sure.

By this time he was sinking the pints: I could see that he

had a taste for it. He asked me if I had any plastering work. I declined, as I said I only did groundwork. This didn't stop him asking for my business card. Fast-forward three weeks to the day and my phone rings. How are ya, boy? This is me, Paddy, ya know from the pub in Neasden. The Kerry lad. Oh yes, I said. The man had smelled it!

A contractor had just asked me not an hour earlier to do a load of sand and cement plastering on an old Victorian wall to tie up between two subbies on a project in West London and on more work on a job in East London, too!

I gave him the job. Monday morning 6.30am outside The Crown in Cricklewood. I pulled up in my black Transit at 6.25am. No sign of your man. Then he appeared from a café across from The Crown Hotel with his hair matted down and wet. He got in the passenger door. Jaysus! I roared at him out of frustration. Did you empty a brewery, Paddy? I'd say he came straight from the pub. I was nearly hungover from the fumes off his breath. I warned him. We wouldn't tolerate men coming to work half-f***ing cut. We can get a plasterer anytime anywhere in London, I blasted. OK OK, he responded. Then the excuses started! I just said, It's up to you, if you want a job or not. I don't give a shit. I am accommodating you! Paddy, I enquired, I need your National Insurance number and your UTR tax number. Most people keep that information on them at all times. OK, boy, I will bring it tomorrow, he responded. The next day he said that he forgot it. Then he needed a sub. The subculture that ended in the 80s. Alarm bells rang. I let it slide. The next day: Oh I couldn't find it. Friday: Oh I forgot again. Monday: Jaysus, I forgot.

I told him to get another job. I had enough of his bullshit. OK, he responded, I promise I will have it tomorrow. I had too much going on and this lad was the least of my worries, but he was on my radar for over a week. That spelled walking papers. The next morning I went to the jobsite? He had his name, number and subcontractor's number. Guess what? It was not the first name he gave me. I asked him what's this about. He told me Paddy wasn't his real name. He said he lied. This new name and number were his! I had to take him at his word. He struck me as a funny sort of fellow. He was a lad that craved illicit life and he knew more dodgy people than I would ever know in my whole life. Anyway, he said, Look, I am sorry, boy, but that will be fine. That name and number is kosher. Send it over. It came back all fine. In the 70s and 80s this stuff used to go on wholesale in the industry. A fellow could have three aliases. One lad leaves Britain and sells his details to another lad. Then the buyer can get two incomes or even three incomes from having three subcontractors' numbers. I can only go on what I am told, right?

Anyway, Paddy was a John Doe. He passed. I paid him weekly and returned the tax as I always did. His four weeks' work was coming to a close. Paddy was due his last week's wages! I met him outside a church on the Neasden roundabout and handed him his wages. He was hanging on as if he had something to say. Then he broke into song about how he was going back to Ireland and how he was sorry for all the nonsense! He proceeded to say to me that he had something to tell me. I was not prepared for what he was about to tell me. The hair stood up straight up on the back of my neck when he told me the following… I came back from America when my father took ill, he exclaimed. While I was in Ireland, I got the offer of a job in the council. A nice, cushy number. At the same time, he said he got an offer of a job in London from a less than scrupulous fellow who happened to own a pub somewhere in London. But first you have to drive a van back to London for me. Now, it has two big Bank of England safes in it. I think it was a Renault Trafic van. Paddy accepted the offer and agreed to drive the van back to England for a chance of a job in London, not to mention for the job for the fellow from Belfast.

Shit usually hits the fan when the wheel falls off the van!
There you had it. Paddy was **set up** to drive the van to England with the safes in the back. Empty they were. They were to be sold to another Irish fellow in Ireland who backed out of the deal at the last minute. All a bit dodgy! The owner of the van was going to be driving his own car ahead of Paddy and doing the journey to London, too! Paddy noticed halfway to Rosslare in Ireland that the driver's side front hub and wheel were loose and about to fall off. He called the owner and told him. When they got to the boat everything was forgotten: a pint was had on the ferry and then sleep.

The ferry doors were open and it was time to disembark. The owner of the van reassured Paddy to just drive on and it will be fine. We will stop at a place a hundred or so miles away from the port and get it fixed. Paddy was driving along the M4 motorway and then bang: the wheel fell off. Paddy careered across the motorway into the path of oncoming traffic. He was creamed by a rigid lorry. The Bank of England safes were strewn all over the motorway. Paddy was in the shit! He cut his leg and had a few cuts and abrasions on his face but nothing serious. No one else was injured. The Polish rigid lorry driver that creamed Paddy was in a shocked state. Anyway, in the midst of all the commotion both motorways were at a standstill. The police sirens were wailing in the distance and Paddy was a bit sore. An articulated truck driver from Northern Ireland pulled up. He questioned Paddy. What happened here? Paddy explained about the wheel and the crash etc… The driver of the truck enquired, Who owns the van? Oh, this Kerry fella, was Paddy's response. Are you taxed and insured enquired the truck driver? Ah I don't know, said stupid Paddy. Should he not have enquired before he ever put his bum on the seat of the van? OK said the truck driver.

You have two choices, boy. (A) You can stick around and face the music. You can hear trouble is on the way. At this point the sirens were approaching fast and there was a chopper in the air in the distance, too! You can stick around and face the music. If you do stay, you will be in the Old Bailey in the morning and you will go down for two years minimum.

Or (B) You can just well, fuck off!

Paddy decided to fuck off. He walked down the service lane of the motorway and ran up an embankment and down through fields. He said that it started to turn dark which helped him evade capture by the authorities. He had to cross a small river. He threw his phone across to a point by a tree. He waded across the small river and made his way towards street lights further up the motorway. He called the owner of the van to return and pick him up. He hid under a street light as he maintained it hid his body heat from the heat sensors of the chopper which was flying up and down the motorway looking for him. The body heat thing he learned from the TV programme "COPS" when he was in the US. The song goes, bad boys, bad boys what ya gonna do, what you gonna do when they come for you? I am sure he was humming away the tune while waiting under the public light.

The truck driver took his number and kept him informed of the goings-on back at the scene of the accident that he absconded from. A far more punishable offence. Two is now probably ten years. The driver told them that the cops were looking intently at the safes and they were trying to open them. The guy who owned the safes laughed and said, "Tell 'em I have the keys." If they can find me!

Oh, and guess what? Paddy left his bag of belongings and his, er, passport and driver's licence after him. What a plank!

There were police looking for him in London, Ireland and probably America. The guy who previously owned the van was being questioned about it the next morning when the Old Bill turned up on his doorstep in London. Apparently, the guy in the car had done some paper swaps to not claim ownership on the van. The previous owner was still the registered owner but he didn't know it.

How complicated and yes, this guy Paddy was a fugitive and he decided to lay all this on me the day he is leaving. Well, at least he gave me his tax number and informed me it was him or it could have been a whole lot worse. It could have been someone else! At the point when he finished the story, I would say all the blood drained out of my face and he says, Are you alright, boy? Ya look a bit white! OMG… I was a bit nauseous. I was shocked into silence! I didn't expect that at all.

London
MORE LONDON CHARACTERS

The Naughty Boys: Used car dealers to skip merchants
There would always be naughty fellows around these yards where I had my tools and materials stored. If these naughties operated near you, they would never go into your space, though. It was an unwritten rule. If you were a keep-to-yourself fellow, they might fear you. They needed a space to operate just like you. The great thing was there were many businesses that supplied tyres, mechanics services, paint jobs and the like. If you were in a yard like this you would be able to get a fellow to fix a compressor or do a paint job for small money.

Anyway. Then there were those who were doing, say, criminal stuff. The authorities would blitz the place every now and again. The Customs and Excise would turn the place over now and then and dip every fuel tank in the yard. There might be 200 businesses there in total. Then there were car salesmen. Some of their stock may not be kosher. There would be a big blitz and then you might catch a glance of two lads being bundled into a paddy wagon and being driven away from a yard selling high-end cars. Might I add in handcuffs and at speed. It was either the cars or what was hidden in them. Wanted!

Although I had nothing to hide, days like that were not pleasant days and very intimidating, to say the least. Squad cars, jeeps and police everywhere. Not very nice. Then a few days of whispering. A few stories going around and then…

The two boys would be back on their forecourt like nothing had happened and then about two months later: gone! The whole place would be cleared overnight. Not a trace left!

The skip companies and a few more naughty boys, not to mention the illegals…

There were also a few skip companies that operated out of these places and every now and then the Home Office officers and a paddy wagon would blitz the place and you would see a few illegals jumping the hoarding and running down the railway tracks to evade the authorities. Real rock n' roll stuff. Some of these guys lived in those dirty yards. No showers. Nothing but a broken-down, old shed for them to sleep in. A life less than ordinary for these boys!

The Naughty boys do get away with stuff! You can see things on the surface but not the second dimension. Nobody really knows the underworld…. and those that do are always borderline paranoid. They live with that fear!

More Naughties - The unscrupulous:
Unfortunately, there are just a few unscrupulous in our business, too. They annoy me intensely. I have no time for these boys. You should be honourable. Jack used to say to me to do a job well or, well, f*** off. That unfortunately is not how our industry works.

I heard from a friend of a friend about a fellow in London who was a less than scrupulous sort of guy. I never had any dealings with him, thank God. I just heard through the grapevine this is what this fellow is up to. He was the kind of guy who would not pay his men or suppliers. He would put his address on his website. It would be some other contractors' address. He had five addresses himself. He had two aliases. The bailiffs would arrive at different doors, including at the office of a main contractor. He would come to the office himself unannounced, demanding his letters. Apparently, he left the HMRC VAT man short. A mortal sin.

He then bust the companies and then started another couple of companies in other people's names. He made the mistake of leaving a few Albanian subcontractors short of money. That was his downfall. Leaving the Albanian mob short. Don't try this at home. That's where a whole lot of trouble started for him. They found him and pounced in the middle of the night. They made him transfer a top of the range, high-powered SUV into their name that night. Apparently he took a little punishment too. Ouch! I would say he was lucky to get away with his life. He then employed other nationality people and then started not paying them, too. An absolute flake! Apparently he is still at it but looks dishevelled and a fraction of the guy he once was. What a waste of a life. Having to maintain two memories is not an ideal way to live. They guy had no scruples. He was heading down the banisters of life with the splinters facing the wrong way. Time will tell a lot.....some day his balls will be in a sling.

Chapter 16

London

JUST A FEW COLOURFUL CHARACTERS WHO I
MET...

Jon V Basilli – The bold Bosnian.
Jon Basilli, or Magore, as the Albanians called him. Magore
is 'donkey' in Albanian. They called him that because he was
as rough as shit. He was a Bosnian peasant farmer before the
Serbians invaded their country. He had a friend, Baz. Baz was
also Bosnian. He was lazy but overall a nice guy. Baz never
spoke about home. Jon and Baz got caught up in the conflict in
former Yugoslavia. John was a sniper for the Bosnian Peoples
Liberation Army. His job was to take out the commanding
officers when the Serbian Army descended on a town. He was
apparently very accurate and he killed a lot of them. There was
a story of where he took out a commander of a battalion from
an elevated position and what ensued can only be described as
carnage.

There was chaos amongst the Serbian Army after John took
out their commander. The Serbian army radio'd for assistance
and two jets were scrambled. The success of the hit on the

commander got the better of Jon and he started taking more and more army personnel out from his elevated position. His own commanding officer was screaming at him that they needed to vacate the thick forest that they were occupying. At the last minute he heard a distant whistling sound and left his position. He was gone about five minutes and the area of hilltop he was occupying was completely decimated. The Serbs lit it up like a Christmas tree.

He was seriously affected by the war. He was a character, though. More like a dog than a cat. A bit rough around the edges. Baz, on the other hand, was a cat. He had little to say! If you mentioned the war he wouldn't answer you. He saw the Serbs burn down his village and kill the men, one of whom was a very old man and neighbour. A rough subject. Jon was a mad fucker. He broke more machines and crashed more trucks than anyone in the firm collectively since its inception.

He was a smooth-talker, though. One time I brought all the men for a few beers up to the West End for a bit of a bonding session. I saw this as an opportunity to get the men to bond, work better and care a bit more about the work. Jon had an eye for the women. I saw him chat up this beautiful barmaid in this Central London pub in Covent Garden. She was having none of it. By the time it was time to go home she was smiling at him, exchanging phone numbers and a date was agreed. He would start by calling them 'darling' in a very seductive accent. It wouldn't take long to reel them in. He had very fixed brown eyes. He was a child really, but get the fuck out of there if he loses the head. My name was Guv'nor. Everything was alright this, and alright that, Guv. He would fuck up regularly. He had a habit of fucking up. He really didn't give a shit. Tony the Boss would call him into the office to have words. He would say shit to him like I am sorry, Guv. I am fucked up since the war. Sorry, and I didn't mean it. The boss would rile him yeah but that was long ago and well this is England, Jon. Last warning. Then the next day he was whistling out the window at some woman at the lights while sitting in the company truck. On a Friday after that meeting with the boss he left the fuel pump open when filling the van with diesel in the yard. He forgot to turn it off and left the yard. The diesel ran across the yard and into the canal and the oil tank was empty. It was only on Sunday the local people realised that the ducks were turned upside down in the canal that was the colour of the rainbow that they traced the damage to our yard. 1000 gallons of diesel gone. Monday morning was a shit storm with the EPA flashing badges and threatening all sorts. I would say that Jon created more complaint phone calls to that company than anyone in its entire history. From Bosnian freedom fighter to a London lunatic, that was Jon !

Chapter 17

London

MONDAY MORNINGS, ROB AND THE
UNMERCIFUL HANGOVER.

Rob was a County Limerick man. We used to collect Rob every morning in South Harrow. He was a lad in his mid-twenties. He was a country boy but as wild as they come. A shuttering carpenter by trade. He was a section foreman for the firm. He was mad for the fast life. Big money, drink and girls. He was always trying to get this cracking barmaid that worked in a North London pub into bed. We would pull up outside the police station on a Monday morning to collect Rob. Rob would be sitting on the floor of this red public telephone box asleep with his legs holding the door open. The windows fogged up. Completely hung-over.

Rob would be still blocked from the night before. We would pull up beside the phone box and blow the horn full pelt. You would see him jump directly onto his feet with fright and everyone in the van would be in bits laughing. It was so funny. It was the same every Monday morning and possibly every Friday, too! The Northern Irish van driver would be calling,

Come on, Rob are you coming or not? Hurry! Rob would drag his arse into the van and start by sighing, Oh I am dyin', oh I am dyin'. The Northern Irish lad would be quizzing him. Were you anywhere interestin' last night? Rob would say, No, only the Shibin. Anyone interesting there last night? No, only that big subbie McDay, talking shite through his broken teeth while showering the pub with spit. His donkey was parked arseways again, referring to Mc Days Roller parked half on the footpath and half on the road. Drunk-driving it home was a badge of honour.

Oh, Jaysus, I am trying to get that barmaid into bed. She won't have it. I am determined that soon she will be mine!

He would then sigh with a kind of painful noise. Then he would bust out a major ripper of a fart. Oh Lord, lads, that Arthur Guinness is speaking to me again this morning. Then this almighty corrosive smell would engulf the van. Enough to melt the windows and singe every hair in your nostrils. There were two Indian lads from Punjab. Our concrete gang no less. Two great fellows. Hard workers. They used to sit in the second row of seats behind the front bench where the driver sat. They would be on their mobile phones running multiple businesses while on their way to work to pour concrete for us. They would in their "angang" twanging accent start hitting Rob in the head shouting, you a smelly Irishman, Rob! Rob would return, don't be hitting me, you jigglies, referring to the way they move their head when they speak. At that Rob would say, Hang on, hang on, there, now ladines, wait for it, Johnjoe, as he used to call one Indian lad. I hear a mini-Guinness is on the way. Oh wait for it, and then a big scuttery ripper and then, Oh Jaysus, well, now, lads, that's a relief. No point in keeping it to myself. Caring is sharing, Johnjoe. Two sniffs of that and you're being a greedy little bastard. Let the rest of the lads have some! The Indians and the rest of the occupants of the van would all be empty-retching and shouting abuse. The windows down and the freezing cold air absolutely cutting us.

Then Rob would yawn and then fall asleep. He would have annoyed pretty much everyone. The windows would be down all the way to work, including about a half an hour doing 90mph on the M25 motorway. It was warmer outside when we all piled out of the van at the jobsite. In the evening Rob used to insist that we go into a petrol station to get the Nuts magazine and a Magnum ice cream. Then we would be in traffic on the M25 and he would be looking at the centrefolds of naked models and the people in the cars beside us in the traffic would be horrified. He didn't give a fiddlers f***. He would put the centrefold up to the window to anyone and give the thumbs-up. The women occupants of the other cars would look in disgust and shake their heads. That was pure entertainment to Rob.

The Minibus on the M25

One day on the way to work we almost got totalled by a rigid lorry that decided to take a left turn too late into a filter road to leave the motorway. He drove us down the filter road, too! We were lucky. 15 men in the van and Polish Paweł the 25-stone, 6' 7" giant inside the back door.

Big Polish Paweł

At the same time we had a problem with the driver's side hub that we didn't know about because Paweł, the 25-stone Polish man, used to sit inside the back door of the van when we collected him in Harrow. When he would get in the front of the van it would lift up. If I was driving the van you would feel the van lift. Really feel it! The van would glide to work. I'd say the front wheels were barely touching the road. The day Paweł was missing the van almost caught fire because the hub was rubbing so much. We got to the site and it was almost ready to catch fire. Panic and laughter in equal measure while we drove to the site. The smell of burning was so bad we thought we would die of smoke inhalation before we got to work. We thought we would be stranded on the motorway with a burned-out minibus. We got to the site and the van hub was smouldering.

We still had to get home. That evening before we left the site we changed the wheel. We had to load about five men into two seats inside the back door of the van to match Paweł's weight to allow us to get home.

Radek the Polish Loon and the vanIncident: Just another normal work day. Not!

We had a Polish carpenter called Radek. He was a bit of a loose cannon. One day we were doing a construction job in Southend-on-Sea. It was the middle of January, snowing hard all day and f***ing freezing. That wet cold that gets right into your bones. My hands were frozen and tingling. We put down the day in the snow while shuttering up ground beams. Five o'clock couldn't come around quickly enough. We changed and got into the van that we had been warming up for about a half-hour beforehand. We were off. I drove to three different jobs dropping men off that morning. My day started at 3.30am that morning. Radek insisted that he drive home. Another sound man, Darek, said I should let him drive. You must be tired. I was tired and agreed. I was on the road since 4am.

We exited the site and this fellow started driving the van like a Formula One driver. I told him to calm down, that it wasn't our van and it's freezing. He kind of agreed with a grunt of a nod. I corrected him twice more in the next ten minutes. In the end I fell asleep as we got onto the motorway. After about a half-hour I woke up when the van swerved abruptly. Remember freezing conditions and heavy snow on the motorway. I was still sleepy and when I looked out the window to my right I could see all the traffic at a standstill and we were travelling at about 60mph. Then I realised that we were in the breakdown lane. I lost it. I absolutely lost the wig. I started shouting at this lunatic. I was roaring at him to slow down. He kept going. He completely ignored me. He continued to drive like that all the way home only with a little more care. Eventually, I woke big Darek and said, "talk to this fool". He is going to get us killed or pinched by the authorities. When Darek roared he calmed down a bit. He was moaning that we wouldn't get home till 10pm if he didn't jump the traffic.

I held my fear/temper until I got to the yard. I was pent up with adrenaline. When the van came to a stop without warning I jumped out, went to the driver's door and opened it. I caught a hold of this Polish fellow Radek and pulled him out of the van and went to box seven bells out of him for endangering our lives on the motorway. It was hair-raising stuff. It was his non-conformance and dismissal of me that drove me over the edge. Big Darek, who was a huge man, intervened and eventually pulled me off him. That little bastard was lucky. It is amazing what fear and anger can do to a man. He got the message. He never put a foot wrong again in front of me!

I often wonder what drives these maniacs! Is it their lack of empathy, understanding or their scant regard for the law!? We might never find out. In a million years I would never do such stupid things.

London
STORIES OF WHEN THINGS GO WRONG!

Story 1
Eddie Jackson and not filling the headings correctly. For those who don't know what I mean that means not packing concrete around the sewer pipes in the tunnel. Eddie Jackson was a great tunneller. He was excellent at digging but he was a bitch for the drink. The lad had a real taste for brandy. He would arrive in a yard at 5.30 in the morning with the shakes. Have his cup of tea and a slice of toast. Then he would recover. One week I caught him not backfilling around a pipe in a heading that he installed 5 metres below a street in the West End. He got irate with me when I gave out yards to him. It was a real shitfest of a shouting match. At the tail-end of the row he said to me, what are the

171

next shower of bastards going to do when we are gone? We have to leave them a small amount of work to do. By that he meant we have to leave them the work of fixing his shoddy work! Here was the fallout. About a year later, I had moved on from that job and I heard through the grapevine that a bus in Kent collapsed into a road when pulling into a bus stop. The bus was empty. It was a write-off. He should have listened to me!

Story 2

This prompts me to tell the events of a concrete frame that was being built in South London. Not my job! There was an old building either side of the new building. When the men got to the top of the building they had to shutter up what they call a shear wall. They put the one-sided shutter up and the steel cage was tied inside. The concrete gang were told that the concrete was to be poured in a controlled manner. The other side of the shutter was a brick wall so it wouldn't take a huge amount of pressure from the concrete. The men were given strict instructions to pour only 600mm in height of concrete at a time and wait for it to go off. Then pour the next 600mm section. In their less than appropriate wisdom they poured the concrete to the top of the shutter.

It held for a while but when they started to vibrate the concrete, the concrete disappeared at speed out of the shutter. They suspected that part of the wall had given way to the pressure. They went next door and gained entry to the building. The concrete had entered the apartment on the top floor of the building. Their suspicions were confirmed when they saw concrete oozing out the front door of it when they arrived at the top of the stairs. Squeaky bum moment! The upshot of it was the concrete had leaked into every room of the top-floor adjoining flat. An expensive misjudgement by the concrete gang. Explain that to the homeowner. Then the clean-up. Men, buckets and a lot of mess. When shit like this happens you must act fast to contain the monetary and legal costs! Quick thinking and offers win The clean-up and return must be done within a few days. If not, the cost will spiral out of control.

Story 3

The day that the grout truck arrived to a job in Central London beside a theatre. The theatre in question had a big opening night for a new West End show. The piling in this big construction project was complete. All that was left was to fill a void between the new piles and the building next door. The grout lorry arrived. The men started pouring the grout into this thin void between the piles and the Victorian building. This is what happened. There were fissures in some of the bricks and joints. The pressure of the grout penetrated the perished voids and pissed into the building next door unknown to the fools pouring it. It was only when the foreman came and asked how many metres had gone into the hole, and the men said 7m³ that they realised there was something wrong. The foreman went into the theatre next door. What met him would be enough to cause you to empty your bowels into your trousers. The grout had pissed into the area just below the stage. There were about 6 inches of fast-setting grout on the lovely regal carpet. Lovely.

Cut to the next scene. 30 men with buckets in a chain getting rid of the grout by hand. Shovels, brushes, carpet up. A new carpet laid in an emergency. The theatre opened that night with a lovely smell of cement. I would love to have been a fly on the wall of the negotiation for the cost of getting out of that one. Phew!

London

THE OLD SCHOOL LONDON SUBBIE, THE ESCORT AGENCY LADIES AND THE PAY-OFF

There may be stuff added on here! Shush...
The story of the old-school West of Ireland subbie. He was a sound enough fellow as long as you worked your nuts off for him. Fair and paid well. This one day we were back in the office and I was doing the time sheets for close to 100 men we had on this particular job.

The subbie returned to his desk in the office from being out running around to all the jobs all day. He put his feet on the desk. He had £200 shoes on him with both socks visible out through each sole and cufflinks on his expensive-looking shirt.

He was a great guy! I learned a lot from him including what I learned on this next assignment.

He was keeping his end of the deal for all the prompt payments by some construction professionals working for a main contractor. The developer arranged for a launch night for the professional construction staff that built the project. The main contractor's boys in charge of the project asked for a favour in return for the prompt payments. There is never any eye candy at these events. This had to be arranged by yours truly.

The same fellow asked me to do him a favour. I was curious as to what the job entailed. I had to take four tickets to the gantry of a boat with a private function on it. The place, "The Thames near Westminster". The deal was I was to meet a girl called Sylvia and give her the four tickets and an envelope. By feeling the envelope, I would estimate it contained not far off a grand in it. I went to the location and saw these four absolutely stunning Eastern supermodels laughing and giggling amongst themselves. Fall off your bike stuff! Drop-dead gorgeous birds. Guinness fart Rob would have loved to be with me. Summer's evening on the Thames and then a glimpse of a bit of eye candy. I approached and asked, which one of you is Sylvia? One dark-haired beauty emerged with that red for danger lipstick on perfectly formed lips. They broke the mould when they made this Eastern European beauty.

Wow! I thought as the heart skipped just a few beats. Focus, Paddy, focus. I am, she smiled. The other three were giggling and giving that hello smile. I almost forgot what I was doing. I was to inform them of the guys who they were to be mingling with. These guys work for the main contractor. You know who you are now, ladies, don't you? You are working in finance and IT in the city, I announced. The girl said, No problem. We are professionals. Exactly, I said.

Here are the four entry tickets and here is the envelope. Good luck. Sylvia kind of put her hand on my shoulder while running her fingers on my cheek. My heart now actually stopped! Are you not coming, too? she purred. No, I said. I turned swiftly just in case I decided to change my mind and started to walk away up the gantry. Discipline, Patrick, discipline. I do remember doing a double take. I just walked up the embankment and shook my head. WOW! Jaysus, it is a different set-up alright. Only in London. I was used to being in the thick of hassle on the site and then an errant like this one? I joked with the contractor afterwards that if he had any more of them jobs, I would be delighted to help. Once those ladies turned away from me that was their business. Whatever those boys did afterwards was on their own meter. We only paid for looky no touchy. What happens after that is someone else's business. What happens in London stays in London. Awright!

London

The London subbie and the less than scrupulous scrap merchant

I worked for this subbie once. He was an alright fellow, to be honest. He used to do an old-fashioned barter with this scrap merchant. The barter was that the scrap merchant used to give him skips for free and my man the subbie used to do concrete work and maybe an odd bit of fencing for him.

A fair deal. This scrap merchant was a geezer from East London. Started off as a barrow boy on the fruit markets. He apparently had a friend in the bank that was of his own ilk. He had gone to the bank and basically asked his friend for a loan of, we will say, 1 million quid. The friend arranged the loan but left out the personal guarantee or accidentally lost it. The guy borrowed the money. Then he stopped the repayments. The bank started to request repayment of the loan. They called in the loan. The friend was fired. When it came down to the brass tacks of it all, the guy basically got away with not repaying the loan at all. The bank didn't have a leg to stand on.

I came into contact with this scrap merchant fellow. He was a guy with the sentiment of the Kray twins. I didn't get a great vibe off this guy. He was definitely an East End villain. I was tasked as part of the barter to do a small extension onto his house. On the first morning, I arrived there were big, eight-foot-tall gates. There were cameras everywhere and then when I did get inside them gates, sliding bar shutters on the windows. More like Pentonville Prison than a mansion.

He was a right old geezer. All the chat. Tough as old boots, geezer accent kind of a fellow. A Guy Ritchie film sort of villain. I met him and shook hands with him. The hair was definitely dyed. We chatted about the job. I advised him on weathering the house next door. I could see from the way he closed up the extension of the house next door that he was not to be messed with. Some relation owned the house next door. I think that it was sold. Maybe it was an acrimonious sale? There were blocks built up on the carpet of a concrete step of the house next door. I knew that it was not a great project to be working on from the outset, but I needed the job.

I advised him to tank the area with bitumen-based membrane to stop ground water from going from his property to theirs. He said, Fuck 'em. I argued with him. What do you mean, 'fuck 'em'? If water enters their house from your land you will lose a court battle on the grounds of nuisance. He said, I still say fuck 'em.

I turned to the main contractor and said, I am out of here. I don't want this job. The East End geezer started by saying, What the fuck is wrong with you? I responded, I am no cowboy, you either do it or I am out of here. He responded, All you Irish are emotional sorts. The contractor I was working for smoothed it over. He took the hit for purchasing the membrane. The next day, I had to ask for a loan of a mini-grinder from the geezer. Our mini-grinder packed up. He gave it to me and said, I want it back. I said, of course I will return it. Anyway, the men used the grinder for a few hours and wrapped it up and I dutifully returned it to the top shelf of his garage and then locked the garage.

It was a Friday and I was returning to Ireland as I did every month. The phone rang when I was on the M11 motorway to Stansted Airport. The subbie I was working for was on the line saying the scrap merchant was on to him roaring that he wanted to kill me. He said you took his grinder! I responded, it's on the top shelf in his garage. Tell him to check. I want a return call from you to confirm. I was paranoid that one of our own might have pinched it. I didn't hear any more back. I rang the guy again to see if he found it. He did. My weekend was ruined.

I arrived back to work on Monday morning and this fellow was going to work. He walked out past me and said, Good morning, as though nothing had happened. You are joking, right? Good morning. More like sorry for accusing and sorry for saying you will kill me.

He responded in rough rhetoric, Hey, keep your hair on. I kept up the aggression. Keep my hair on. Nobody has ever, ever, accused me of stealing. How dare you! Finger pointing and expletives in abundance. It was like water off a duck's back to the fella.

I think it sank in eventually. Are we alright again? Have I settled the score? Good, I said. Let's start again. Good morning, dickhead. Most people were actually terrified of this fellow. Not a nice character at all.

Our work was done and then this Irish carpenter was finally fitting a kitchen in the scrap merchant's house. He was a diligent fellow. The day was an absolute scorcher of a summer's day. The scrap merchant's wife said to the lad and his son. You can go for a swim in the pool if you wish. They declined about five times, knowing the type of guy the villain of a husband was. They eventually gave in to the lady's offer. She gave them the husband's trunks. That wasn't bad enough but then she decided to go shopping and left a big, aggressive dog the size of a horse out while she went to the shops. The two boys were in the pool and then tried to get out. The dog who was frothing at the mouth wouldn't let them out of the pool. Call me sceptical but it did occur to me that the scrap merchant himself told the wife to do it. He was probably watching these two tits panicking on his CCTV cameras from his scrapyard office. Watching them trying to exit the pool, he was probably getting a great laugh out of it. Eventually she came home. The two boys changed at record speed and headed for the gate, suffering from shock. Not a nice experience. They were right to run. But hey, don't swim in Al Capone's pool without permission or YOU MIGHT END UP BEING BURIED AT THE BOTTOM OF THE GARDEN.

London

The London Concrete Frames Subbie: A day in the Life
I was working for a concrete frames subcontractor in London in 2010. It is tough being a small concrete frames contractor in London. Few make it! It will command every ounce of energy you have and it will take minimum 18 hours a day from you. You can't be a shrinking violet in this game. It takes real leadership, balls of steel and absolutely no f***ing fear when things go wrong. That happens daily. Being a project manager in charge of a big concrete frame for a small subbie can be a tad challenging. It was 2010 and the economy was in shit. I was working for a pair of subcontractors who were, by all accounts, decent fellows. The job was priced tight to stay in the game! They were growing in size as a company so they had tight prices to keep the company pulse.

They had about 180 men at this stage and were doing jobs that were about three times the size of what the company could manage all over London in order to stay in the game. Construction rates were in the doldrums and every contractor was fighting for the same business. They were in true Irish fashion growing the company in millions by the year. This is always a dangerous time as your expenses and problems are growing fast while your resources are depleting. A tough balance and your energy levels must be high to absorb the constant barrage of pressure.

I was managing this site that had at its peak about 150 men on it. The main contractor had about three safety men just going around site all day trying to catch men standing on a guard rail or just doing something silly. They would then issue a yellow card. If you got two yellows it was immediate dismissal.

I was doing 18-hour days some days to try to keep up with the speed of the project. I would arrive at 7 in the morning to find 10 to 15 lads on the site with problems. Steel drawings not tallying, the shuttering didn't arrive, discrepancies in the drawing dimensions, or some guy dropped something from an upper floor the day before, and there is a pile of paperwork and formalities to be dealt with in order to resolve the issue.

Every Wednesday there would be a big concrete pour. On Tuesday, I would be up to 90 trying to ensure the deck was ready for the big concrete pour. The penalty for being late would be £10,000 per day. It had to go ahead. The Scottish guys doing the post-tensioning cables (real Jocks) and our Romanian steel-fixing subbie would be having a bargy about being in each other's way. Real mental stuff. Hard fought battles. Threats from either party of walking off the job. I would have to quell the unrest. It might take a half-hour to get them to calm down and resolve the matter. The senior engineer would be breaking my nuts about some irrelevant stuff. This didn't even warrant a blink of your eye. Madness.

We had to sign off a pour form sheet before the pour would be sanctioned. He would be saying that the pour will not go ahead unless I appeased him on his requests. I would then have to take about 20 men from another side of the job for an hour to install extra props or something to satisfy him. The concrete plant batcher would be calling me PANICKING, "Why are we not pouring?" There would be seven wagons (56m^3) of concrete waiting on this fellow to give us the green light. I would be having a shouting match with this young (senior) engineer. The concrete pump operator and my Indian concrete gang would be pouring expletives on me. Panic would be setting in as they would be worried that they would lose daylight and that the concrete pour would go into the early hours of the next morning. The concrete plants rotation of returning trucks would be now in the toilet. This would leave long periods between pumping. This would cause other problems. The concrete that would still be on the walls of the concrete pipes would be going off. This would restrict the flow. All because this inexperienced fellow was enforcing his position and silliness!

Every evening when I would go to bed from those jobs I would be waking hourly. Did I remember this or that? In the end I got a notepad beside the bed and wrote whatever was in my mind. An odd morning, I would wake up in a sweat. The 300 thoughts a minute gets to you. It's a game I gave two years of my life. I enjoyed it in many ways and then got out. The main contractors we worked for had a zero target on accidents. This made it hard to make progress. They had all the power. They would be breaking our balls. This would put more pressure on us.

They would be living in hope that we would go bust so they wouldn't have to pay us. It's a cruel business!.

The deliveries were challenging. The main contractor's forklift driver was retired to looking out the window in the compound. He was safe there. In the finish, I used to get a Donegal fellow with a 45-ton excavator to unload the deliveries for us. No language barrier or fooling. I would offer him £50 by throwing a red one in the door of the machine and telling him to unload it while his foreman had gone to the other side of the site. 20 minutes it would take him to unload the entire 40ft trailer. The guy I worked for would be screaming down the phone at me, Is that wagon unloaded? It is costing me £300 a load a penalty for waiting time! Then that artic would pull off-site and another would arrive. The same story. The Donegal man would be called again. As soon as your foreman disappears get that load off.

The Indians strikers. Lost in translation and the floor not exactly tallying! Bristol

The Indian boys from Punjab were our concrete gang. A brilliant bunch of lads. They also struck the formwork after the concrete floor was poured and then did the back-propping. One day I marked the floor with blue line-marker spray. This line was where they were to stop striking the deck. I was in the office and our engineer, a brilliant polished English fellow, arrived in the office. He came into the office worried and in a rush. He said that he just did a check on levels of first-floor slabs D and Z. There was a 25mm difference in height at the pour strip. Straight away I knew what had happened. The Indians forgot about the blue line and kept striking the deck. The floor slab had started to bend ever so slightly. I had to get them to use brute force to push it back up into position. The good thing was that they hadn't gone far. The floor wasn't compromised. Static hair moment.

Chapter 18

London

MI5, THE BLACK PHOTOGRAPHER AND THE
FERMANAGH FOREMAN

I was refurbishing this park in Vauxhall Central London for a
good friend of mine. He was a main contractor in London and
he had a lot of council contracts. He was a fellow who kept my
company in work.

The jobsite was near the National Crime Agency and not
a stone's throw from the Houses of Parliament. Not only
is England the most watched place on the planet but also,
anywhere close to MI5, MI6 or the Houses of Parliament. There
are more cameras than brickwork. Both the crime agency and
5 and 6 were right beside us. We as ordinary construction
workers were being watched closely. That's the nature of the
beast.

One day while we were on this site I did see about four top
of the chart Range Rover SUVs pull out of this one-way street
that had a few railway arch garages at one end. It was a quiet
one way street. Hardly anything went in or out of the place.
That made me think a little about secret doors and entrances

for the intelligence service... Then I thought that my face recognition was done and I, along with my workforce, were clocked by the boys upstairs.

One day these North of England lads arrived to do some work on the roof of one of the nearby tower blocks. They were not very friendly. They told us they were going to have to park their van in our construction site. I, of course, obliged as I would anyway. We think that they were undercover police technicians. They were wearing grey boiler suits and they were apparently installing intel antennae on the roof of these buildings. Possibly MI6... or so I thought. My thoughts were compounded one day when a photographer turned up. He was taking photos of the street for a high-profile developer so he could make a photomontage of the finished development.

I invited him into our job if he wanted better photos. He declined but then asked me if I knew that the building behind him is the National Crime Agency. I said that I did. He proceeded to tell this story, that he was walking up that side street where the gate is for the vehicles to the enter the building. He was about to take a photo when this guy appeared out of the security cabin and warned him to refrain from taking photos. Apparently MI5 or MI6 rang the security guard and told him to interrogate the photographer. He looked a bit shaken. White with fear. I, on the other hand, knew London was a place with many hidden secrets and a hierarchy that one could only wish to see.

The plot thickens. We were working closely with a charity to help young people into work. This included construction apprentice hopefuls and media students. We had a half-dozen of these pre-apprentices on-site.

The media student in this case was a black guy with a bit of a history. There are plenty of white fellows with history too. The guy used to come to site to video the young guys at work for a few hours a day. This was for a project they were going to present to the council. One day I received a telephone call from my foreman Pat, a Northern Irish fellow who was usually as cool as a breeze. This day he was not himself. He was a bit agitated. He was speaking at a hundred miles an hour and said the police are here on the site and they are **lifting** the photographer. His words were. They are arresting this buck and it's all a bit rough. It was chaos!

They said they are going to lift us, too, if we know him or anything... The "Special Branch" boys are asking me for an answer. I had ten men on that job so I said, Tell them we don't know him, but tell them he works for the said charity. The phone went dead. I rang him an hour later. He answered. Aye, that was rough. His words: these bucks had earpieces, were about 6ft 8" and they were in plain clothes. It was only then we realised that the intel masts could belong to the intelligence service and they were watching the black fellow and got spooked about his motivation and decided to lift him. He was released with no charge or apology for that matter. If the powers that be want you, they will get you. No question about it! It all happens in London. Never underestimate the resolve or power of the British establishment.

London

THE BANKSMAN AND THE SHAKEDOWN THAT LED TO THE PISS BOTTLE

The crane driver and the banksman on a particular job in Finsbury Park that I was doing a concrete frame on were giving me a bit of hassle. They were being uncooperative, to say the least. They were complaining about everything. They were the two guys who were serving us with concrete, steel, shuttering and the rest. We were the only contractor on-site. They were playing up. I called my boss and told him that these two cockney geezers were not conforming. It's too windy. We are having our break. Sorry, Pat, I am not doing this and sorry, mate, I am not going to do anything you ask, mate, because of the way you ask. I am in charge of the crane, mate, and I decide. A load of bullshit. It was all a game with these two. The job was now suffering. The Guv'nor sent a boy around. Call him the guillotine man. A bag man of sorts. He called the banksman aside and told him to get the crane driver down out of the crane and meet him in the stores in ten minutes. The banksman was quizzing me, what is this about? I responded, only you know the answer to that one! I was asked to observe by this boy who was sent to the job, for reasons unknown to me! Ahem… The two boys went into the tool store container.

Our boy started to explain that Paddy here (me) was having a bit of bovver with you two boys, right? They went all defensive. The guy deviated the conversation to lead them into a false sense of security. He said, Well, now, lads, we need a crane that operates well on this site. We need concrete poured as regular as clockwork. We need you boys to work with us on it. I will offer you the crane driver £200 every Thursday evening as a sweetener and you the banksman £100 every Thursday, too! They first said, No, mate. Then they accepted the money. I thought, this is new to me. They accepted the first instalment. Our boy then asks me, did you see what I saw? I responded, Yes. What did you see? he asked. I saw you giving these two boys money. Correct! Now, he continued, you boys just blackmailed our company for money, a kickback. We now own you and if you get lairy again with Pat we can now get you sacked off the job. We have two lads already lined up to take your jobs. He continued: We work every day until 6pm at the earliest and we also work through lunch. Do what you are asked. I don't give a fiddler's if it's blowing a hurricane or chucking it down, you keep going! He then said to the crane driver, bring two 2 litre empty bottles with you every day. You won't be coming down out of that crane for as much as a piss. Awright, boys, that will be all. See you next Thursday. I have a feeling that it is all going to work out. Talk about their plan backfiring and talk about a hustle. That's London, baby!

London

THE STORY OF FLORIN THE ROMANIAN, THE
TRAVELLER MICKEY CONNORS AND THE POLICE
RAID

Florin, an immigrant from Romania, came to London as a
16-year-old with no papers. He, like other immigrants, used to
wait on Chichele Road in Cricklewood or outside Selco for a
contractor to pull up and give them a day's work.

Day 1. Mickey Connors pulls up this random morning and
takes him and three other Romanians with him for about £60
each per day, or so he says. He takes them to an abandoned
granary building like an old mill house. He gives them a load
of grinders, petrol saws and cutting equipment. He tells them
to cut every bit of copper, lead and anything brass out of the
building, including wire.

Mickey had a good day on the first day: at least three runs
of copper with about a ton in weight at a time. £3000 per ton.

Day 2. They are back and cutting as though their life
depended on it. The young Romanians were suspicious that
things were not altogether right. Mickey was missing for long
periods. Another good day for Mickey and day two was done.

Day 3. Three words. Shit, hit, fan! This day Mickey had
headed away with the first load of wire. He was gone off-site
for ages. A couple of hours in fact. The fella had the sixth sense.
The boys stopped working and took time for a sandwich. While
looking out the window they observed Mickey returning. He
drove into this parking area and didn't return to his usual spot.

Instead he drove his van down to another gate and parked inside it, facing out. Then out of the blue the police in paddy wagons sped into the yard. Mickey took off like a bat out of hell in his Transit Tipper Truck. The cops raided the building and the three young fellows were arrested. They didn't know anything, only that their employer's name was Mickey.

They were complaining that they were not paid for the work and they didn't know anything. The police let them go after they realised the young guys had been duped.

Then for the finale. Mickey turns up the next morning to collect another few boys for work again. He gave the young 16-year-old Florin a bollocking about his tools. The police had confiscated them. The young'fellow had balls and challenged him about payment for the three days and their transport. The traveller said, How can I pay you for a job that you never finished? Talk about neck and the sheer lack of empathy or remorse.

That's the thing: there are real toerags of people like this in this world!

London.
DAILY TRIP TO THE TARMAC PLANT IN WEMBLEY

Arse out of your trousers stuff
During my early days as a subcontractor in London I had taken on these jobs that were bigger than the value of my company. I had bitten off more than I could chew in true Irish style. I did

the deal on a handshake. Again, I hadn't a whole pile of money at the time. I had a few grand in the bank and I got the chance of doing this job in West London. I took it. I, along with a good few lads, did that job but not without some pain.

The way it works if you order, say, three tons of 20mm base course tarmacadam to be delivered in a 16-ton truck payload, you pay the full £100 for the 3 tons and then £50 per ton for the other 13 uncarried tons. You are charged for 13 tons of airspace. £950 for 3 tons which would cost £300. No way, I hadn't the money! I had to do this job in increments, as the client would only allow us to do two entrances to these apartment blocks at a time. A fellow might collect 2.5 ton of tarmac three times a day in a van that could only legally carry one ton! Either 6mm wearing course or 20mm base course.

A few weeks earlier I was stopped by a policeman driving a paddy wagon. I was at the traffic lights and I could see him in the middle lane two cars back. I drove away from the lights slowly, and as I picked up speed the cop did the same action. I slowed down a bit and then he did until he was holding up the fast-moving traffic in the middle lane. He then put on the lights and raced past me. He ordered me to pull into the next slip road. He then brought me to a weighbridge with what seemed a normal load. I was only carrying a few fence panels. He maintained that I was 60kgs overweight. He fined me and gave me three points on my licence. He wasn't too bad but he still nailed me.

After that episode, I decided to get bigger springs on the back of the van so no matter what load was on-board it would be hard to detect if it was overweight by just looking at the van. The fellow I had driving the van wouldn't be stopped. Call me naughty but then again so were those bastards that nicked my vans and broke up the last job. Nobody rescued me then! Where were these coppers then when I was on my uppers!

The tarmac plant had many characters collecting tar. They would first break the rules by dieseling up the body of the pick-up with diesel and a brush so that no tarmacadam would stick to the steel body. There would be signs littered all over the place prohibiting such an act on the grounds of the health of the environment. This didn't stop some idiots doing it anyway. Then they would sometimes line up wrong under the hopper which was about 6 metres higher than the bed of the truck. A novice would park the van incorrectly and then get the tarmac or concrete on the roof of the cab of the van.

I had a lot of fun watching the antics of these boys. It was pure entertainment. There was always a lad trying to fit three types of tarmac into his truck. A real Jaysus moment. He would be making funny angles when parking under the hopper. Sometimes hitting the steel framework of the batching plant. Then the guy who was doing the batching would come out of his office waving and shouting expletive after expletive. The men collecting the tar didn't give a shit!

Driving through the lights at Hanger Lane and sweating bullets...

After I got the big springs on the van, I thought it would only be prudent to test them. Better to be hung for a sheep rather than a lamb. I would get my lads to collect the load of tarmac from the plant in Wembley. The load was a big payload. He would drive around the A406 North Circular Road and head for Hanger Lane. This is a very busy roundabout/gyratory. The road at the lights heading for Ealing starts to gradually incline into a hill. He told me he used to be sweating bullets when going towards the traffic lights and hope that they were green. If the traffic lights were not green as he approached, he would slow down until they turned green. He would floor the accelerator of the van going up that hill for fear that it would cut out. If it stopped it would never go or start again. If the van stalled on the road, well, then, he would be going away in cuffs. I have to say that I never asked him to ever attempt this again once that job finished. It nearly killed us both. I sweated bullets daily for six weeks. The work commitments and the safe delivery of the job meant more to me. The price of perseverance got me over the line on that job with my shirt and underpants unsoiled.

LONDON
LONDON JOBS: SONG 2

When you start a construction business in London from nothing you have to do all manner of jobs and you see the bizarre, the crazy, the rich, the scrapyards and the storage yards. You meet the Arthur Daleys of the world and then there is you. Where do you fit into this world? The environment is rough and the speed of life can be overwhelming at times.

There I am in a house of the richest man of a big country.

He didn't become that for being straight or for that matter soft. A military man no less. There I was standing in his house in London facing two American architects flown in from Washington to discuss what they wanted me to do regarding a building services survey. The house was one of the smallest houses on a road in Kensington. It was a mere 25,000 square feet over five floors. It had a servant's stairs and quarters. Odd job was a Chinaman and the guy looking after the house. The janitor, as you would call him, with a bowl haircut and a knack for bowing at you. I was waiting for him to produce the steel hat. A nice man but he was watching you like Goldfinger's apprentice. He would appear in a room and then bow as he was leaving. After a day I didn't bother taking notice. Always offering you curry. A decent fellow.

To win the job the Jewish architect, asked me, "How many days will it take to complete the job?" I said, it will take three men three full days to complete the survey. This was a very fair assessment. He quickly retorted, I think it will take three men two days. I returned, I am not interested in the job anymore.

My friend, the businessman who brought me there, and was also the guy who was pricing the job for them, was saying, Let's not be hesitant, while squeezing my forearm. I stood my ground. I said, if this man can do all this carefully in two days with three men and protect the carpets that have an inch and a half pile on them and walls that are papered with gold, well, then off you go. The Jewish man backed down. I said, You flew in from America this morning. I live in London. I know this city and the workforce. You don't.

I thought, Well, that went well. We are now definitely out. To my amazement he spoke up. When can you start? I said, Monday. He said, Why not tomorrow? I refused to answer. Then he asked the suited and booted contractor, can we have contractors' all-risk insurance? This fellow had been up at 4 in the morning had the worm and was ready to eat our worm, too. The contractor friend of mine said that he would only provide PL and EL insurance to the value of £15 million. The Jewish lad was not happy. I said that if I hit a pipe and the water flowed down the wall the contractors' all-risk would cover the entire £20 million refurbishment job. Not a hope. We started to head to the door. My fellow said, we will send on a quote and we will start on Monday if you are agreeable.

Fast-forward a couple of minutes. We are passing the gates of Roman Abramovich's house and my man, a very accomplished businessman, asked, What should we charge for that job? I said, Well, I will want 3k plus VAT. In which case you will need 5k. If you want to make a few bob charge more. The next morning he called me back and said we got the job, Monday morning and it's 4k for you. Well done. A good negotiation. It took three days, no nonsense, although I sweated a little. We didn't hit any services but I must admit the mechanical and electrical spec was better than The Dorchester hotel. Unbelievable for a domestic building. I really got a glimpse of how the other half live. Unreal stuff!

London
LANCASTER GATE

I got another subcontracting job in London in Lancaster Gate. It was a job to do enabling work in an old hotel ironically called Leinster House. Although there was probably more work done in this Leinster house than the one in Dublin. The building was six floors over a basement and it consisted of three massive town houses joined together. It was this enormous building that you could really get lost in. The guy who owned it was a Middle Eastern prince or something... Some Virgin Islands company was the beneficiary of the proceeds. Another fiddle, I suspect. We were called in to do some substantial work on it in order to extend the planning. The bombshell was that we had a week to complete substantial works and we needed about two weeks. The owner was trying to flog it for £42 million. Pocket change! A contractor from Shannon in Co. Clare did the brickwork for us. A legend with a fast and furious bunch of brickies.

This piece of property was a valuable piece of real estate to be leaving idle to gather dust. This was one hell of an ornate building. The detail in the cornices and the cast-iron balustrade of the stairs was exceptional. This building was the height of opulence in its day in the 1870s. The basement was quite dark and cold, even though it was lit up with lights. You got a sense that there was a presence there. Ghosts of Christmas past, if you know what I mean!

This building was on an amazing street with lines of Victorian columns painted in Portland white. In the evening, before I would leave this building for home. I would sit in the office on the first floor which was a room about 60ft long x 30ft wide with 13ft high ceilings. It was huge. I would sit and look out those high French doors that led out to the French veranda. I would observe the tourists passing and the high-end cars purring past. Bugattis, Lamborghinis, Rollers and all of that glitz. It was silent in the building. I could feel what it was like to be a lord or lady who lived there during really gentrified Victorian times. Pure luxury. Then a whisper of a thought: Why is it when you go to Heaven all the interesting people are not there? Who said this?....

Tea cosies and incorrect information!
This morning a fellow pulls up in a Bugatti Veyron car and jumps out. He has a tea cosy as a hat. Working for a man with black gold. Arab money!

That was the thing about London. I saw a whole different side to London from being in the presence of the super-rich property owners to being on the high-rise sites where the Indians were pouring the concrete, the Romanians were doing the shuttering and steel fixing, and the Irish were running the big subcontracting companies. Then to scrapyards which is a whole other dimension of a world. Daley, the yard letting agent, and the boys in the skips business. If you want to make it in London you have to be a bit of a naughty, wayward fellow. No room for honest Joe's here. But it can be what you want it to be. There are opportunities. But you have to be careful. Be very careful in this town. This is where the tea cosy man excels!

The guy in the Bugatti Veyron was a freelance salesman for the owner. He was a fellow dressed in a habit with a crocheted tea cosy on his head. He was wearing a pair of black trousers under the habit and a pair of Reebok runners. A naff necklace. He had a geezer accent. A bit of a Middle Eastern Del Boy.

Then these two very well turned out, suited and booted, high-powered bank officials came to view the building. Potential buyers. I could overhear the guy talking to these fellows. He was talking absolute rubbish. He hadn't a clue what he was talking about. I was cringing. I didn't know much about this building but the little information I had would have sold it. Manning a showhouse at 16 years old helped me conclude the cluelessness. They were asking him simple fundamental questions about planning permission and the current state of the building and ownership. He gave a load of waffly answers. He was out of his depth but he was the guy driving the Bugatti!

Then about an hour later this well-dressed lady arrived and she looked like a potential purchaser. She was dripping with gold. I asked her not to go into the basement as we had construction work going on down there. Then she started asking me a load of questions. I said that we are only the subcontractors here. We don't know anything about the legal status or the current planning. We are only contracted in to do remedial work and site investigation. She followed me around the building trying to get information. I gave her the surveyor's telephone number and told her that's it. She kept haranguing me for information.

In the end the tea cosy man returned! It turned out to be

his wife. She was trying to collect all the information from me because this fly-by-seat of your pants fellow was on a wing and a prayer trying to sell the building! My man Pat the gangerman, the 4am man, would have done the job of selling that building standing on his head. Pat should have had the Bugatti and the tea cosy! Although that would look a bit odd back around Fermanagh… What a world…

chapter 19

London

FRITH STREET, THE ALOOF GERMAN, THE NINE-
INCH PARTY WALL, THE CHAMPAGNE-SPILLING
GEEZER AND THE HALF-NAKED BIRD

I know what you are thinking. It's a very long, arduous
description. It will all come to light, I promise. If you stand in
Piccadilly Circus and you look to the right of the sign there is a
street called Shaftesbury Avenue. Walk up that street and after
a few hundred metres turn left and you are in Soho. Walk down
Frith Street and when you meet the Cat and Pheasant pub you
are there. We will call it that for privacy reasons!

On a Tuesday afternoon I received a call from an Irish
main contractor. He asked me to meet him and this German
client in Soho in the morning. It was Wednesday morning. I
met him. We entered this building that a less than scrupulous
German fellow owned. I did my homework the night before. I
telephoned a connected construction friend of mine and asked
him, do you know anything about this building? The word on
the street was that z German was not to be trusted. A colleague
had done some remedial work in the building nine months

earlier and he was still unpaid.

That's the thing, you must be very aware of who you are working for in London. An unscrupulous fellow can lead you up the garden path and then sink you. Two weeks was my limit. I had a buffer. The main contractor was the guy who was working for the German. Not me! I had a two-week turnaround on the money agreed with the Irish contractor. I warned him about this fellow. They were pricing the whole contract. £10 million, I heard. I said, If you never got the contract it would be a blessing.

When we went in through the whitewashed glass front doors, there was a Barclays pay-as-you-go bike hanging from the ceiling joists. It had been spray-painted pink and had some Christmas silver tinsel wrapped around it. All done by the anarchists that had broken into the building some months earlier. They had pictures of The Queen in her Jubilee attire and crown with 'Fascist' and a swastika superimposed onto it. They also had pictures of David Cameron on the wall with a hatchet in his head superimposed onto the photo with a caption, "the best cut of all". In the basement there were two wheelie bins with a plywood potty on top on them and they were full to the top with excrement. 'His' and 'Hers' written on the lids of the bins. The pigeons had taken the top floor of the building. A real hell-hole of a place.

The building was half stripped out. There were lights and electrical cables remaining in the building with Eastern European plugs on them. I learned something in Poland. In my estimation I would say there was some cheap labour imported from Poland to do the soft strip out of the building. It looked like they left in a hurry. We met this German fellow Clous who worked for the Kraut. This fellow Clous was asking me a lot of questions. He was really going at it with the questions. He asked for a business card. I gave him my one. I then asked for his. He gave me a card belonging to someone else in the company and then scribbled out the numbers, wrote his number down and then scribbled it out again and handed me the card. Real weird stuff. Then it was my turn. Who owns the building? Where does he live in Germany? I will be requesting payment upfront. I then told him I had done my research on them and it wasn't good. I would say Clous z German never met a fellow like me. He could have been the Guy himself incognito! I also informed him, I have never not been paid in London. I always get paid, if you know what I mean, and I pressed the card back into his chest and we teamed up with the building surveyor and the contracts manager.

CLOUS AND THE KEYS!

The key-cutting shop incident

I agreed that I would start the next morning, but we need keys. We took a walk around the corner and straight into the key-cutting shop. Clous hands over the key to the keysmith. He said, two of them please. The keysmith was a proper Londoner. He did the keys and then hit Clous for the money. Ten pounds please, mate. Clous hands him ten euro. You take euro? No, mate, this is England. Come on, £10. We take cards, too! Clous made out he had no c(h)ards, no p(h)ounds. I stepped in and paid the £10. I was going to be charging Clous £20. All the time my research was being confirmed. I had the key. Clous and his building surveyor left us. I warned the contractor. This guy is a skinflint and you will earn it here.

The following day I passed a building directly behind our building while getting some coffee for my hard-working crew and the music was absolutely belting out. There was a larger-than-life London geezer carrying a bit of weight with his mates. He was swinging out with this near-naked stripper bird at 11 in the morning while spilling his £300 bottle of champagne all over the floor. My lads not 9" away on the other side of the wall were in shit and digging like hell. Diesel fumes and a smoke-filled basement v champagne and scantily clad birds. Which would you rather? If they could see what was going on just a few inches away they would have jacked up the job in search of a similar setting. What goes on behind closed doors or party walls in London only God really knows!

THE UNITED COLORS OF BENETTON GIRL

Earlier that morning!
Compressor set up, hoses sent down to the basement. I had an Angolan man and a few Irish fellows from Kerry busy at work. I parked up my van and upon my return this young, 20-something girl was ready to enter the building. I caught her. I asked her if I could help her. She was dressed in every colour of the rainbow and she was as bold as brass. I at first couldn't take her seriously.

She had all sorts of earrings on her face and purple hair. She had a thick book in her hand and alluded to it as the party wall agreement. Oh yes, I responded. She then started into a tirade of heavy-handed, aggressive rhetoric threatening that we were breaking the rules of the agreement. WO WO WO, I replied. Calm down. I just arrived! I have done nothing wrong here. She erupted into an ultimatum. She said that I could basically work the 60lb hammer for an hour a day. Ridiculous!

My mind again was calculating: there was trouble here before! Anarchists and foreign contractors that left in a hurry. I pleaded with her to let me operate the pneumatic hammers for a max of five hours a day. She had to get permission! Then she reluctantly agreed. I told her in exchange for that we would have all our survey done by the following Wednesday. Cut to the next day. The concrete was like flint so I was stretching the boundaries of the agreement. I wanted out by the next Wednesday, too. I was going to make no money if I had any surprises. We had a few surprises already, not including Clous z German. Our job was to break out concrete in the basement and dig trial pits and record where the footings of the building were located. In one instance we found at the corner of a chimney that there was no wall two feet below the finished floor. Paddy had been here before. He had set up a steel beam under the floor over a fulcrum of a concrete pad. He then had poured a concrete floor over the steel beam to make it act as a cantilever. This cantilever was holding up four floors of a building. Essentially the basement floor was holding up the party wall!

Kerry Brian and the pub floor

What this meant was that the four storeys were being held up by the weight of the floor. When we saw this development we were sweating bullets. I decided to stop work in this area. The engineer came and went white. I calmed him down. He requested that we dig in where the brickwork should be and see if it was only one skin of brick that was missing. The brickwork was completely blown out. I would safely say it was a war wound from the Blitz in '41. I instructed Kerry Brian to continue digging. When we returned to see how he was progressing, he was under the basement floor of the pub next door and he said to us, There is no wall here, boy, in his Kerry accent. We nearly collapsed with fright. We roared in sync, Get the fuck out of there, you fool! Not a funny experience.

On that same job I hit a vein of an old underground stream. When you are in a hurry to get a job done, that is usually when things go tits up. The trial pit filled about a metre high in about two minutes. I never thought it was possible to backfill that hole as fast with sticky clay in order to plug the hole. I nearly shit my pants. We could have flooded the basements in the whole street if that water kept coming out of that vein. Phew! It was flowing like a river and the ground around the hole or around the water orifice was breaking up quickly. A London Irish fellow used to work with me had a saying when things were going tits up: Another squeaky bum moment, Paddy! We solved that one, but just in the nick of time. If I didn't plug that hole in quick time, I was absolutely finished. Flooded basements and a big enquiry. The lady with the funny hairstyle would be in line to give me a good caning if it went wrong. In the pub, there would be kegs floating up to the basement ceiling etc.

The final word on this job is that when we were backfilling the trial pits in the basement, I got a push from another dimension. I had a shovel in hand myself. Pressure to get finished. I decided to backfill this one hole in the corner of the basement. I started backfilling and then whoosh. I felt this cold energy and the next thing you know I am in the bottom of the three-metre-deep hole on my head. I never got out of a hole as quickly. My hair was standing firmly up on my head. It is very disarming when this happens to you. Heart rate going through the roof etc… That happened once before on a job in Ireland. I guess it was a person from the past that was not happy with us being in their space. Ghosts, Clous z German, pigeons, the girl with the purple hair and Boris's bike! You never know who or what you will meet in construction in London… eh.

Chapter 20

Poland

PADDY WENT TO POLAND BEFORE THE
FINANCIAL BUST AND SAW THE DARK SIDE OF
THE MOON! I WANTED TO KEEP GOING IN THE
CONSTRUCTION BUSINESS SO I LOOKED EAST.

The East is just different. It was a Communist country so there is a dark side, too. In most cases the people are stern in appearance. They are generally alright once you get to know them. It is a very nice country and they are collectively very hard-working and decent people. The food is good and the cities are clean and friendly. Kraków is a great weekend holiday destination. If you are a young fellow looking for a wife you could do worse than a Polish wife! They strike me as a smart nation of people. They are programmed to think outside the box. For me it was a great distraction, experience and education.

Paddy Poland…
At least that's what my Irish friends called me. The economy in Ireland was overheating and the price of land was not

sustainable. We were in a bit of a pickle. There was a correction coming. So, Paddy headed for Poland. My friends said," Is that not arse about face?". Sure, the Polish are coming here and you are going there! The thing is, their economy was in better health than the Irish one. The Polish economy was less exposed to the sub-prime market. They were a clever bunch of people. I employed cleverer people to advise me on my business affairs while I was there. This leads me to the almost land acquisition and the Polish Mob.

The Polish mob. A weird event! I worked this one out from the outset

Land on the German border. The Polish mob. A very close call! The young, scared legal intern. The flea market, "literally". The very weird hotel. 7ft tattoed bald men with squinty eyes. Ladies of the night. A whole lot of Irish bottle. Balls of steel. What a total f***ing kerfuffle. Don't ever harbour an idea to buy cheap land in Eastern Europe online!

I was trying to secure the purchase of some land in Poland for construction and development purposes. I had tried the big cities but hadn't much luck purchasing sites there as there was a lot of red tape and a few naughty boys, i.e. estate agents, bringing you to a piece of land that was landlocked and 2km away from the nearest utility service! I was happy buying some apartments in the city to refurbish as a learning curve. I decided to look further for land. I looked on the internet and found some interesting plots of land that were zoned for commercial use on the border with Germany. These sites were cheap and close to main arterial roads. Alarm bells did ring a little regarding the price.

The following week I flew into the city of Wrocław and picked up the young lawyer, Degera. Degera was my translator. She was a 20-something, sharp, young lady with a stern business attitude. Young but educated and smart.

We headed for the border to meet what we didn't know was the head of the mafia in this region. We were early so I asked Degera to ask the local people at this border town market how was business. They were not very friendly but answered the questions, saying that years earlier the market was better and now it was tough. The rise in value of the złoty had made a difference to German buyers. I should have twigged that the lack of friendliness was as a result of what was happening in the wider community. We stopped into this hotel to get a bite to eat. It looked clean and tidy with one car in the car park. We nevertheless walked into the hotel and there was nobody on at the reception desk. Then out of the blue this guy appeared. We asked about lunch. He started to open the restaurant and turn on lights. There were no guests in the hotel. We politely left. Too weird for me. It would have been hours before we would have been served.

Upon leaving the hotel, there were women walking along the road waving at us when we were driving from this area to the motorway. They were waving at me and I back at them. Degera broke into song that I shouldn't be waving at these young ladies. She explained that they were ladies of the night. I was to be honest a bit amused and laughed. When I realised it was true I was equally shocked. It's midday and these birds were touting for business. I thought, this country has a lot of hidden stuff. We went to the location of the site to meet the vendor. This silver Opel Frontera SUV appeared in the entrance of the field. This short fellow about 5' 4" got out of the SUV.

He looked like Paulie the Villain in *The Sopranos*. He was wearing a 1970s canary yellow shirt with wide lapels, brown pinstriped trousers and crocodile skin cowboy boots. Jaysus, I thought this is a blast from the past. He looked like the 1970s New York gangster Carlito. I immediately knew this fellow was a shady character. I got a cold vibe from him. I just knew he wasn't right. The eyes always tell a lot!

He beckoned us into his SUV where he spoke to my translator in harsh, clipped tones. He started to drive around this field and then he said that the land is zoned for a hotel. Like the one we saw up the road, I thought. He then took us to another site saying it was zoned for a petrol station, but his friend in the local gmina (council) could sort it so we could get anything on the land. Alarm bells were ringing loud. I stayed cool, not making eye contact with the intern as I didn't want her to lose her nerve as he was an intimidating sort. He drove us off at speed to speak to his friends who ran the council. He stopped at this cigarette kiosk with 'Zigaretten' written on the roof of it. It was at the side of the main road. This is a joke, right? We waited in the car while this headbanger got out to speak with his friends. Three big fellas emerged from the kiosk. They had scars, no hair, tattoos and the look of convicts.

The young lady started panicking. She whispered to me they are the mafia. I told her to keep cool. I told her to tell him when he comes back that we want to buy the first site we saw (the hotel site). I would just have to confirm it with my accountants in Ireland. But consider the deal done. Without delay she was to tell him that we are late for another meeting in Germany and we must get back to our car. The Germans won't wait. The guy accepted our line about buying the site but was hesitant in returning us to our car

I was worried now as the three boys were hanging around the car looking at us with that bulldog squint. These fellows were probably under surveillance by the authorities. This would be unknown to us, the innocent vendors. How would we get away from these fellows if they suspect we might be undercover cops or something else? I would certainly get away from them, but Degera wouldn't. I got a little thick with him when he wouldn't get moving. I started pointing at my watch and speaking in Irish. He started up the SUV and made his way to our car. We thanked him and told him that we would be putting the offer on paper and he would have it in two days. We got into our car and headed out of there slowly. I took a minute to make a phone call first to not let him think we were fooling him.

We got out of there and headed straight back to the city. The irony about all this is that a month later, Degera called me to tell me that the police blitzed the area. She recognised him on the news being taken into custody. She recognised him by the 1970s dress code and the crocodile skin boots as one of the ringleaders. The story of the young girls waving at us on the road was that they were trafficked from Romania and Bulgaria as sex workers and the locals were forced to give up a bedroom as and when to allow these girls to do the business with a client. The people in this region were scared into submission. The market people were not friendly at all. They were being hustled by these feckers, too! It was, to say the least, an eye-opener and a bit stressful. I can't imagine what would have happened if the guy got paranoid and took a set on us with those three heavies looking on. Someone was definitely praying for me that day!

Poland

WHILE LOOKING FOR INVESTMENTS OR COMPLETING PROJECTS IN POLAND I SAW SOME INTERESTING THINGS. I HAVE COLLECTED A FEW STORIES AND PUT THEM TOGETHER.

The last train to Poznań…

In my wisdom I was a fellow always looking for different opportunities in different places. I decided to go to Poznań by train. Trains in Poland 15 or so years ago were not the most reliable mode of transport. Apart from breaking down regularly they were hunting ground for a few undesirables. The little villains were putting small gas canisters for cooking under the train seats and turning them on, hoping you would fall asleep and then they would rob you. That's why the train passengers were opening the windows. It was minus 30 outside. I was bloody freezing. I, the Irishman, was stomping around the train ordering people to close the windows. When it is minus 30, the windows are open and the train is doing 70mph, well, then a Paddy is going to let the red rag temper out. I didn't give a damn if half the passengers were 7ft, intimidating and irate. I wanted to be able to be reunited with my nads. People argued with me, but I closed the windows anyway.

Then after about two hours the train abruptly pulled into station and a big guard entered the train with what looked like a slobbering Alsatian dog but it was more the size of a pony than a dog. I was half-asleep and then this wet slobber hit me in the face. I nearly hit my head off the roof of the train with fright. This big mutt with a huge muzzle and a big chain around his neck leading to a huge hand of a guy who looked like Richard Kiel or Jaws in the Bond movies. Then another arrived in the carriage from the other end. The naughties were caught. They were probably eaten by the dogs when they got off the train. No harm. An intimidating experience!

Another rule of thumb in Poland is to bring a packed lunch and a flask of tea on the train. If the train breaks down on a journey and you are stranded for, say, seven hours in the dark it's good to have some refreshments to keep you warm. A very nice young lady shared some delicious lamb sandwiches with me on such an occasion. I suspect that life is different in 2019. I am sure that services are excellent and reliable now. A decade ago it was different. Very different!

Poland

THE CRAZY POLISH CHEF

The Polish chef that got off light. I, on the other hand, was a laughing stock when travelling through security at Wrocław Airport with the biggest shiner you could ever imagine. How do I tell the wife…? Picture this. Dimly lit pub, beautiful barmaid smiles at this handsome Irish guy. Me! You can understand how a drugged-up, off-duty chef that had a crush on this lady and a history of violence found this offensive and made it his ambition to try and kill me. He hadn't bargained on meeting a half-cracked ex-rugby player that worked in the construction business and was as strong as an ox. In an unprovoked attack the fellow took a set on me. He decided to hit me head on in the eye full force in a running format. I didn't see it coming. He was hell-bent on killing me. This guy was not going to stop until he killed me. That bar stool weighed about 50kgs. The four leg marks I would say are still on his chest 12 years later. I have to admit I still have a scar under my eye today from that bastard! He has the stool marks, too, I hope!

My left eye was completely closed with the force of the impact and my cheek burst open. There was blood everywhere. My right eye focused and this fellow was moving around me like Muhammad Ali. He was going to have another go. I had to act fast! Rugby definitely saved my life that night. When one eye was closed from the first punch it rose the instinct in me to hit him with the stool. The rugby tackle was for survival. I hit him furiously with the stool first. Eventually I left the stool down as there was a stairs behind him. I didn't want to send him down the stairs on his head. It would be me answering to the police.

I walked away to the bar counter after dropping the stool. This guy was so drugged up that he didn't even feel the effect of the thrust of the stool. Then he walked out over the stool and made a beeline for me again. I had space and distance this time so I returned to that time when I was on the rugby pitch. I tackled that guy with passion and force. I drove him 20 metres across the room, gathering tables and chairs during the fracas. In the end where he fell a load of tables and chairs engulfed him. I took the opportunity to stand on the chairs and tables to put some manners on him. He couldn't get up and it was affecting his breathing. Not breathing is different to not feeling anything. The bar staff eventually intervened. I was lucky. The jumper I had on was blue but it was now red. When I saw myself in the mirror my face and eye were destroyed. The barman gave me a large whiskey to calm the nerves. I drank it and made a run for the stairs. The crazy chef was in the kitchen. I thought, he is probably getting a knife. Lucky Irishman!

Being hustled by 10-year-olds in Central Poznań to paying the utility bills

The day we parked the car in the centre of Poznań and two ten-year-olds accosted us and with words about car theft or damage in the area. If we give them 5 zł each the car would be safe. If not, well, then you are taking a risk. Then the hand was out! My friend from the Polish countryside who wouldn't usually give them the steam of his piss insisted that we both give them money. He also said they are the local mafia boss's kids. They were being primed for a life of crime. I then asked, will the car be OK when I come back? He shrugged his shoulders. Maybe, maybe not. It is better to pay. I was from a family, too, that primed me for a life of construction. I suppose you can't choose your family. Right!?

Paying the utility bills!

Interesting stuff! Queuing up to pay the electricity bills. 2005! It changed afterwards but you would start lining up at 7.30am for a 9am opening. It would take about 30 more minutes to complete the payment and then about ten documents stamped 100 times. Some of the old staff would have done better to say, Fuck off, at the end of the transaction. Sometimes they would send me around the house to a few different hatches. Then some old biddy would say that I couldn't pay the bill now or something as I was maybe a day early. You must conform to the exact rules of the game. I would usually hit the roof as it was two and a half hours after I started queuing up. Then a young lady would sort it all out in five minutes. Communism was still in their psyche. The young 20-somethings were a very good bunch and had great English. They were progressive but the old generation didn't exactly like them. It suited me that the young people were there to help.

The Polish traffic cop and the not so smooth pay-off!
What my Polish friend said about bribing the traffic cops with the €50 note in your top pocket didn't work for me exactly, or did it? I was driving to a small village about 40 miles from the city one Saturday morning as a bit of a diversion from my working week. While driving on this road at a moderate speed of 80km/hr a car came around an oncoming bend on my side of the road. He was swerving all over the road and I would say he was doing about 160km/hr. An absolute lunatic. He flew past me, but not before he flashed his headlights frantically. I naturally thought, What a complete idiot. I came to the bend that he had emerged from and there he was. A suited and booted member of the constabulary. He beckoned me to stop and pull over. I dutifully pulled in.

I rolled down the window. Dzień Dobry, I said. That's hello. Nie mówię po polsku. I don't speak Polish. He started wittering on about documents. Shit! I had left them after me in the hotel in case the car was nicked. My friend had warned me never to leave the documents in the car or you will pay the price of the loss. The cop removed his police hat and left it inside the window. I remember a friend of mine saying that if a cop in Poland holds his hat inside the window with his hand that means a €50 note. If you don't pay the bribe they might lift you. The corruption was rife and I was worried. Remember this fellow was irate, to say the least!

Stupidly, I reached into my pocket and pulled out the wallet. He went absolutely berserk. Then I lost the rag with him. I started shouting at him in English, Will you come out with it, whatever you are trying to say or arrest me or something? He then started shouting at me "Vamoose, Vamoose", while pointing in the direction of the road ahead. I just pulled up the window and fucked off. I didn't give it another thought. I was convinced that by the time I got to the town that I was visiting, I would be pinched. Never heard another thing. It was about the stupidest, foolish shenanigans of a theatrical act that I ever starred in. Another thing I noticed was that the police car was a rust bucket of a polonaise. It wouldn't inspire confidence as being a car of choice in a high-speed chase. If it had another exhaust it may have been mistaken for a wheelbarrow.

Poland
THE MADNESS OF AN ARTICULATED TRUCK DRIVER ON THE WRONG SIDE OF THE ROAD AND BEING CAUGHT IN A BLIZZARD

While overtaking us and 12 other cars that were in front of us, a truck driver decided unwittingly to play chicken with an oncoming car. He had no choice as there was no room for him to pull in. The car in a complete panic to avoid a collision went down an embankment and then luckily emerged while he spread dust all over the road. The driver of the car emerged by the skin of his teeth while skidding erratically all over the road. The truck driver continued unfazed. A road phenomenon in Poland at the time. Lack of care or understanding for basic road safety. People took crazy risks with their lives and that of others. I was seeing Polish trucks and I mean articulated trucks down an embankment or in a field on their side.

When I broached my friend Asia about the story of all these big trucks on their side in a field she just said, "They fell asleep." It didn't seem unusual or out of the ordinary to her. Part of the norm! The country had a horrendous traffic accident record. Speed and overtaking on bad roads were part of the problem. The culture was another part of the problem. A lot of risk-takers! Not an ideal job being a truck driver in Poland. Employers would be making drivers drive for very long periods. The drivers were also stuck in that culture!

One time we got stranded on the motorway in absolutely freezing, blizzard-like conditions. There was an accident 5km ahead. The motorway authorities had difficulty getting the articulated lorry that had jack-knifed on the motorway off the road. The truck had taken out a few vans, a bus and a few dozen cars and they ended up in a pile in the ditch. I think unfortunately there were fatalities. After four or so hours panic starts to set in. People are cold and you have to conserve fuel if you don't have much. The petrol station could be hours away. We were stranded for about six hours. The international truck drivers were getting nervous and were out of their trucks knocking the ice off the tyres regularly with mallets in order to avert them skidding or not even being able to move.

When we did get moving, a Polish translator who was accompanying me and a few others in my car said, You have to let the trucks off first and they will weave slowly across the lanes to break up the snow and ice for us to be able to drive the cars. In fact, that was how they warmed up their tyres. Very interesting stuff!

Our friend maintained that in Poland you should bring a flask of tea, water, blankets and some food in the car in the event of being stranded somewhere in the winter. When in Rome and all that!

My Polish Chauffeur...

This friend of mine collected me from Poznań Airport one time. It was white out. Minus 25 outside. Cold is a polite word. We were on our way from the airport to the hotel we were staying in but not before he showed me his home town. He had converted the car from petrol to LPG gas. It was cheaper. The gas bottle/tank rolling around the boot. On the journey he drove around a bend at speed. The car decided to stall on the railway tracks. Absofuckenlutely nuts! The rave music blearing out of his strap-on cassette recorder. 1990s rave and the train heading for us as we are stuck on the tracks and he was saying it may take some time to start. I then realised that they didn't have any level crossings. You would stop the car and look right and left before crossing the railway tracks. As he drove around this 270-degree bend the car had cut out. The gas bottle moves sometimes in the boot and turns off the engine and then turns it on again. Well, fucken' hurry on, will you!? I was roaring. Then the car starts, I mean with a hundred metres or so from this fast-moving freight train to go and we are away. That was a moment!

Poland

THE TAXI TO KRAKÓW. A HAIR-RAISING EXPERI-
ENCE!

The taxi from Rzeszów to Kraków and the mother doing Hail Marys in the back seat

She was trying to bribe the taxi driver with biscuits in the same manner you get a dog to behave. This was to make the lunatic slow down and drive on the right side of the road… Then there was the old timber bridge we had to wait on halfway through our journey. It moved 2 metres while we waited at a red traffic light that was midway across it. The bridge moved due to an articulated truck that drove up onto the same bridge behind us. We all nearly shit in our pants. The taxi driver didn't seem fazed. There was a concrete bridge being constructed beside this old bridge. I remember being shocked that this was an everyday bridge on a main road! I couldn't fathom that in 2006 this was normal in Europe. Clearly there were parts of Poland that still had Third World infrastructure.

The reason for all this taxi business? you ask

Ryanair left us in this airport seven hours' drive away from our destination as a result of fog. The whole of Central Europe was covered in fog. It was a one in 50 year event. To be fair it was not Ryanair's fault. Upon our arrival at the airport, there were no hire cars, thousands of people asleep on the floor of Rzeszów Airport together with no food, and people beating each other up while trying to mount the only bus Ryanair had organised for thousands of passengers to get you to your destination. FUCK THAT! I saw a taxi and then another. People were making a beeline for these two taxis. I got there first. The first taxi sped off. I asked the second driver, How much for a taxi to Kraków Airport? He said 1000zł (€250). Normally it would be 400zł. I tried to haggle to 600zł. No chance. I can get 1000 złoty, he responded. I pulled eight 100zł notes out and gave them to him. Then I opened the boot and said, Take us to Kraków Airport. He had the money upfront. I put the bags in the boot and got in. He wasn't happy but he was taking the mick. He was mouthing off and then driving erratically and then the Hail Marys started and then the biscuit bribes. So much for the Catholic Irish mammy. It worked. A woman can calm a guy down, too, it seems! He stopped for a piss stop where we were able to corner him and speak a cúpla focal about behaving himself on the road. We drive on the left! This is Poland. Right! You drive on the right. He smiled and started to behave after the telling-off. There was a lack of understanding about your customers' welfare, respect and safety. Road safety was still in the Dark Ages. In the end we got to Kraków Airport. I then drove another six hours to Wrocław on a heavy ice-covered motorway. A crazy experience I am sure all involved will never forget.

The Investors…From Australian men in crocodile boots to drugged-up Iranian nutcases working for Middle Eastern princes!

In the mid-2000s, there were foreigners buying up lots of real estate for exorbitant amounts of money in Poland. There were lots of companies making investments, too! Mergers and acquisitions were commonplace. Driving the market crazy. Foreigners were popular and then not so popular. Remember the Polish chef. The stories we were hearing in the Irish pub was that of the girls, the nightclubs and the drug parties. The place of hangers-on, the gold-diggers and the college girls who just wanted a place to stay while in the city in college. They were willing to trade sex for digs. Ask Rodney the Scouser? He knows all about that one! Every month or two there would be a different one. "This is me girlfriend" will be on his gravestone. He had a saying, 'Live fast, die young, good-looking corpse'. He was definitely on that path of being a good-looking corpse. There were foreign fellows arriving in these popular Polish pubs, late bars and establishments. Men from Portugal, Spain, Iran, Australia, Norway, England, Ireland, Germany, the USA and many other places. Absolutely nuts.

Some of these fellows were doing business for the big boys. Some were young fellows working for oil tycoons and some were working for the oligarchs. These lads would arrive in the pub on a Friday or Saturday night with a harem of women, one better-looking than the other. A whole area would be reserved for these fellows. The champagne would be flowing and then the limos, Ferraris and other top of the range SUVs would pull up. I used to frequent a really funky bar with all the new décor. An amazing venue! The mob definitely owned this joint as they did many other establishments. The manager used to joke with me that it is all about who you know. If you know the right individual and the price is right, well, then it is green lights all the way. I was never invited to the parties, thank God, but I heard a lot about them. Real wolf of wall stuff! Hotel rooms trashed, someone would OD and police would be called, not to mention the old mob and the security boys. All very gauche!

The Norwegian guys!

In a bar one night I met these two Norwegian lads. They told me that they were welder fitters. They were employed by a steel fabrications firm in Norway. A multimillion dollar company no less! They were the two most experienced men in the company. They were sent to improve the standards and introduce new production facilities to the plant in Poland. They had a funny experience while there. They maintained that the company they had bought was a well-run company. The Polish guy ran the place like clockwork but some of the workforce were heavy drinkers. In the mid-2000s the sub was still commonplace here. When they told me I got it immediately. They maintained this Polish director was a social worker as well as a tough boss. The wives would come on an odd day looking for an advance on the husband's wages as he had drunk all the last week's salary. The Polish boss would give the money and when the guy would turn up on, say, a Tuesday he would call him into his office.

He would proceed to give him a dusting down about his behaviour and then tell him that he gave the wife an advance on this week's wages. They guy might erupt in anger. Then he would say, You are fired if I hear any more, now get out to work. Rock and hard place stuff!

In the interim the mother company in Norway was planning

another expansion into the Ukraine. They were interested in another acquisition. The Polish guy was to be their guide and eyes and ears. He was used to life inside the Iron Curtain and he knew the warning signs. When they told him that the company wanted them to look at this steel plant in the Ukraine the guy laughed and said, You have got to be kidding me. That's as good as being in Russia and there is no chance that the local mob will allow you to buy a company without some level of pain. The CEO heard their concerns but ordered the visit. The Polish guy told them, Bring no wallets. Bring a few euro. A few dollars under your foot in your socks and your passport.

Fast-forward to the border. The Polish guy had told them that the border could be tricky. He said you might have to wait a few hours in a traffic jam. It's a fiddle of some sort. They arrived at the border. They lined up behind a single row of traffic. After about 15 minutes a military jeep drove down to them. A border guard walked up to the car window. He asked the Polish guy what they were doing going to the Ukraine with two Norwegian fellows. He responded that they were old friends and they insisted on seeing the sights in the Ukraine. The border cop nodded! Then he took off his hat and held it inside the car window. Do you want to go through fast or slow? The Polish guy knew the drill. €50 dropped into his hat. He put the hat on his head and beckoned them to follow him.

They drove behind the border guard to the front on the line. The cars and trucks behind them were blowing their horns and getting irate. The border cop appeared again and took their passports. Then they had to be x-rayed in a garage that seemed to take an age. They were free to go! They drove into the Ukraine. The two Norwegian lads told me it was bleak. They were 20 miles down the road and a cop pulled them into the side of the road. Another €50 fiddle. As he was dusting them down for a bribe a BMW flew over the top of the hill behind them and then threw into a skid as he saw the cop. He hedged his bets and decided to make a run for it as the cop was out of the car, and floored it. By the time the cop got moving in his clapped out Polonais car the BMW was well gone! They drove off as the cop was gone. They never got the opportunity to leave the poor cop his bribe! Ha.

In the end they were delighted to return from the Ukraine. They said it's no Poland!

Poland
THE YOUNG IRISH PUP (APPRENTICE) AND THE SCRAPE WITH THREE POLISH HOOLIGANS

It all kicked off when we walked from our hotel in a Polish city to the old town centre. Both I and this young apprentice that I brought on a trip to Poland for an Eastern European education walked down this street by the river. We were on our way out for a pint. We had arrived in Poland a few hours earlier. These three hooligans appeared out of nowhere and were coming towards us with bottles of beer in their hands. They looked a bit rough to be honest. I could feel there was going to be trouble. As we were passing them one of them dropped his shoulder and hit me and I stumbled into a skip. Naturally, we thought it was appropriate to have a go at them verbally. Then it all kicked off. They broke their beer bottles and challenged us to a fight. I was concerned, although ready to defend myself.

To my surprise the hooligans got a good run for their money. They had not banked on the little Irish apprentice being harder that a coffin nail and as mad as a box of frogs. He frightened them. I'd say that this young Irish pup had them when he threw a big lump of concrete at them without warning from out of the skip. He followed that with bricks and debris. To my absolute shock they ran off! The fear was in their eyes when the bricks hit the road. But no, that wasn't enough! The apprentice ran out of his zip-up jacket and chased them down a street wearing only a tee shirt. It was about 10 degrees below freezing. I tried to restrain him, but he ran out of his jacket. I never saw fear like it in three 6ft, most intimidating, military-looking chaps. They started the trouble. It was a row that they simply couldn't win. A mad Irish Bruce Lee! He was all over them like a rash. He was beating the stuffing out of them. They were simply apologising and out of breath when I eventually caught up with him. He had given them a right auld hiding. I challenged him about using his loaf/brain and questioned him about what would happen if the authorities arrived. We are in Poland! Right? The Polish police are called to the scene of a fight. What are they going to say?

They are going to say, Oh, the Polish lads started this fight. The police would say, Oh, let's take them bold Polish boys in for questioning. No, they will not! It will be: Let's deport these two thick potato heads to Ireland but not before we unleash some Polish hospitality on them. Let's beat them and break their balls first. I eventually got him to cop on and walk away. His response went like this. You were no F***ING help to me. I had to deal with them Polish tinkers myself. Lightweight. Thank you would suffice. The point of all this is that this pup was on a learning trip. OK, I appreciated him getting rid of these fellows, but he was on an educational trip. Not sure if he was worthy of the step up in employment status!

In the end, I just sighed, I give up! Now can we go for a few quiet pints please? I then had to lay some ground rules with this pup. He eventually apologised!

The estate agent that I saw spades spinning in his eyes

I must admit this incident really freaked me out. I never had such an experience. I knew a Polish estate agent that used to do some lettings for me. He had a partner in business. Then the guy I used to deal with had left the business and this other partner was in his place. I never really liked this partner, but hey ho, I had business to do and that was it. I kid you not, the meeting was like a dream. I mean nightmare…

I had an appointment with him in the meeting room of his office about a pending letting. As I was talking to him his eyes went into a spin with spades in them and his face stuck on a devilish grin. He looked like the joker in Batman. I immediately blinked and then again and then again. Still the same. Then blinked hard again and his face was normal. I couldn't talk. The hair stood on the back of my neck and I left that office wet through. Completely traumatised. I genuinely know what

I saw. As I walked to the lift on the upper floor of this building, I was questioning what I saw. I hadn't taken a drink and I never did drugs. It was one of the scariest things I ever saw. Madness! It was truly a terrifying moment. One I don't want to see again.

Final Chapter.

LIFE! IT'S ALL A GAME. IT'S ALL ABOUT HOW
YOU PLAY IT...

The moral of this story is that I didn't really choose construction.
Construction chose me and I had no way of knowing it on
that day in 1974 when I arrived in this world. You can choose
your friends but you can't choose your family! It was in my
environment and in the blood. My family were in it. The two
male generations before me were born into it and followed it
religiously to the letter! They worked bloody hard. So, for me it
was like being born into a mob family and I was being primed
from an early age for the world of work. Construction work.
The old dog for the hard road and the pup for the path, and
all that stuff. The male family members wanted me to follow
into it. I was eased in. Not! There were times that I absolutely
hated it and times it was a blast. The only really positive thing
I can take from it is that I learned a hell of a lot about people,
construction and life. If you treat people well, even the hardest
bastards will go with you! I could soften tough men with a good
environment, pay and conditions. The men would work hard if
these three things were present. Appreciation and discussions

go far in this world where most people just want to be valued.

What I learned in my life experience to date is that if you are lucky you are born into this world with energy. You have an abundance of it early on in life and it diminishes as you get older. No matter where you are in life you always have the power to change it by the way you think and act. Just look at me thinking I can write a book. Ha!

The construction game as well as other industries are labour-intensive and they will demand all the energy you have. To counter this reality, you must use your energy in a measured and well-thought-out manner in order to get longevity in your career and life. Think and act like you understand that life can be long and that you, too, will get old, and then make a plan, however simple it is. Make a plan and know this, that it is subject to change! You can't keep going at 150mph all the time and not run out of fuel. Take three or four physical burnouts like me and it teaches you. Try to put an old head on young shoulders. It doesn't happen that easily. I only learned the true meaning of this when I turned 40. I was going at construction like a well-oiled machine for close to 25 years when I realised that the body could only take a certain amount of abuse before it showed signs of wear. Rust started setting in on the undercarriage!

Take a car that was manufactured in 1974. If you sit in one, it will most likely smell like leather and it will have that petrol smell. It will show signs of wear. Its shape will have changed slightly and it will need more care and attention. People like me thought in my twenties that I would never get old. I WON'T

BE THAT OLD CAR! It never even crossed my mind what old would be like. At 45 I intend on finding out in another 100 years. As the poteen maker said to me in his early fifties when they dig me up in a couple of hundred years I will look the same as I do now. The poteen being his preservative. I have no doubt that the fellow will live long. He didn't take life seriously and enjoyed the devilment. The comedy contributed to his life expectancy.

In conclusion, this is what I have learned:

A. Work hard like the money doesn't matter. If you do a job for the enjoyment, it isn't work. After all, we need people to do all sorts of jobs to keep the wheel of life turning.

B. Gratitude is the key. Say thanks for the most basic things.

C. Start a pension early on in life. Whatever you can afford.

D. Work is good for your mental health and your sense of being. Look outside the box now and then. Consider your options and know there are no limits. It helps when you gaze into the unknown.

E. Don't take life too seriously, do your best at what you are doing. Aim for the stars and be as happy as you can be. Be kind to your mind! Your mind actually needs rest like your body.

F. If you are lucky you have 80 years on this planet. Work 80 years out in minutes! It will focus you on what you want out of life.

G. Have a huge amount of fun. Take holidays and see this wonderful world and enjoy what the planet has to offer.

Learn more about the galaxy and the world. It is fascinating. Infinite!

H. DO DIFFERENT THINGS EVERY DAY TO MAKE LIFE MORE INTERESTING.

I. Comedy and having fun are wonderful ways of seeking enjoyment and fulfilment. Releasing endorphins in the brain. Ensuring well-being.

J. Natural unobstructed daylight is a key ingredient to a happy and calm home. Cut clutter and live minimalistically. It helps to keep equilibrium and wellness in your life.

If all the above fails – well then, don't call me!